Sometimes people say to Tabitha Brown, "I've never eaten vegan before." As Tab says, "Have you ever eaten an apple?"

After living with a terrible undiagnosed illness for more than a year and a half, Tab was willing to try anything to stop the pain. Inspired by the documentary *What the Health,* she tried a thirty-day vegan challenge—and never looked back. Wanting to inspire others to make changes that might improve their own lives, she started sharing her favorite plant-based recipes in her signature warm voice with thousands, and now millions, of online fans.

Tab's recipes are flexible, creative, and filled with encouragement, so you trust yourself to cook food the way it makes *you* happy. If you're already a "cooking from the spirit" sort of person, you'll love how much freedom Tab gives to make these delicious vegan dishes your own. If you're newer to cooking—or to vegan cooking—Tab will help you get comfortable in the kitchen and, most important, have fun doing it!

In this joyful book, Tab shares personal stories, inspirational "Tabisms," and more than eighty easy, family-friendly recipes, including:

- Yam Halves Topped with Maple-Cinnamon Pecan Glaze
- Stuffed Avocado
- Jackfruit Pot Roast
- Crab-less Cakes with Spicy Tartar Sauce
- Who Made the Potato Salad?
- Kale and Raspberry Salad
- Strawberry Cheesecake Cups

Cooking from the Spirit is for anyone interested in plant-based eating and all lovers of food, plus anyone who wants a little warm inspiration in their lives. As Tab says, "Honey, now let's go on and get to cooking from the spirit. Yes? Very good!"

COOKING
FROM THE SPIRIT

EASY, DELICIOUS, AND JOYFUL
PLANT-BASED INSPIRATIONS

TABITHA BROWN

PHOTOGRAPHY BY MATT ARMENDARIZ

WM
WILLIAM MORROW
An Imprint of HarperCollinsPublishers

To my fans,
who continue to
love and support me
in the kitchen—
thank you.
This is for you.

contents

Introduction ix

breakfast & brunch
1

pizza & good stuff
21

burgers, sandwiches
& tacos   43

appetizers & sides
69

main dishes
99

soups & salads
133

sweet treats
& fresh juices   159

Introduction

Hello there. I am so happy we're here. It's the moment you and I have both been waiting on. I wanted to make sure I didn't just give you a cookbook, but me in the form of a cookbook, so it would feel like we are in the kitchen together. So thank you for your patience, honey. Well, with that being said, let's get into it.

Cooking is love, it's friends, it's family. Food is just so amazing in how much it holds, how many memories, how many feelings. It has all this power in it. But also, food and cooking saved my life. I was very sick for a year and a half. One day I got a headache in the back of my head that rested back there for one year and seven months. My body was attacking itself, and my doctors couldn't figure out how to fix it.

Then I watched the documentary *What the Health* and decided then and there to go on a vegan challenge for thirty days. I originally did it for my health. But the advantages extended so far beyond just my headache disappearing. It not only healed me—it changed my entire life!

What Does It Mean to Eat Vegan?

First things first: Vegan food is just *food*. When I hear people say, "Oooo, I hate vegan food," I think, *Really*?? You hate apples, pickles, blueberries, strawberries, rice, beans, potatoes??

Retrain your thinking around this concept, and don't get stuck on the word "vegan." In fact, lots of people just say they eat a plant-based diet. The point is, don't let the word stop you from considering something that could change your life—like it did mine—before you think about what it really means. The list of what you do eat as a vegan is so much longer than the list of what you don't eat. A vegan, plant-based lifestyle *excludes* animal products of any kind, meaning anything made with meat, fish, dairy, eggs, or honey. Everything else is yours for the eating. You can have every vegetable, every fruit, every grain, every bean, every legume, every nut and seed.

If the mere thought of changing what you eat makes your shoulders and stomach tighten up, if you suddenly feel like you need to protect everything about your diet and change nothing, especially not the meat and fish and cheese you eat now, it's okay, there's no pressure, but I want you to take some deep breaths. Don't think of it as losing something, but rather as gaining something new. Go ahead, take a few more deep breaths. I'll be here when you're done.

Listen, when we get afraid of stuff related to food, it's because we put so much thought into eating. We put more thought into food than we do most things. Sometimes when people hear that I'm vegan, they express a lot of disbelief and, strangely enough, worry. I often wonder why people didn't express the same worry about what I was eating when I was sick. I think it all comes down to us resetting our minds sometimes—how we think, where we put our focus. It starts with what we put in our body, but it's really in your mind that the reset happens.

When I first started my vegan journey, suddenly I met so many "doctors" I'd never known were doctors. All sorts of people came out of the woodwork giving me advice and warning me about "dangers." Be mindful of these folks; don't let them distract you or discourage you. You focus on what feels right to you. If you want to try vegan eating for thirty days, go ahead and try it for thirty days. Don't listen to the people telling you that you won't get enough protein. The folks saying that probably couldn't tell you what amount of protein is "enough," anyway.

One of the biggest misconceptions about a plant-based lifestyle is that vegans don't get enough protein. I don't know why this is such a trigger for folks, but I am asked about it all the time. Before I was vegan, I was never asked if I was getting enough protein. On a plant-based lifestyle, we get our protein from the same place that cows get theirs: plants! Crazy but true, right? Seriously, plant-based foods—leafy greens, beans, quinoa, seeds, nuts, the list goes on—have all the protein we need.

So if you're interested in trying a plant-based lifestyle, just take it one day at a time, even one meal at a time. There's no right and no wrong. Start by doing the things that feel comfortable to you. Don't be hard on yourself. Life is hard enough. We don't want food to be part of the hard. Be gentle with yourself.

Transitioning the Family to Veganism

Another question I get asked all the time is how I got my whole family to join me in this vegan lifestyle. Honey, I made it taste good! And I took it slowly.

I think it's a mistake to try to transition your family to a plant-based diet unless they make the decision to do so. Simply make amazing meals and allow them to try them with you, but don't force it. If your family is on board for the new journey, start with some traditional nonvegan favorites that can be made vegan, so no one feels like something is missing.

At the beginning, I still cooked chicken and fish for my husband and kids, but everything else I prepared was vegan. I focused less on what I was taking away and more on what I was adding, and I made sure those sides and extras were really delicious. At the same time, I was swapping out our pantry and refrigerator staples and replacing them with vegan options. So I made their grits with vegan butter and their grilled cheese with vegan cheese. I added nutritional yeast to pastas for a cheesy flavor. They didn't even notice. Kids, especially, often just don't know the difference.

I certainly wasn't advertising that the new dishes were *vegan*. I was just serving food to my family like always. And I let them all make their own decisions. If they didn't like it, I didn't force it. As they got comfortable with what they were eating, and even began to request my vegan versions of things, I talked to them a little about how nourishing the food is. When we know better, we do better, right? I'm thankful for what I've learned and want to share it, but only when people are ready to hear it.

As for processed foods, whether vegan or not, I've always tried to minimize them. But when my husband was on his vegan journey, he craved things like turkey sausage, and I was so glad to find great substitutes made by companies like Field Roast and

Beyond Meat. When you are new to the vegan journey, sometimes you just wanna know you won't miss out on your family favorites. I call it walking into a new journey like you've been there before! A few dishes in this book, such as Nachos (page 102), Chance's Sausage and Veggie Pasta (page 118), and Country-Style Steak with Gravy (page 121), came from our early days of eating vegan. There are some other dishes that were favorites in my family from the very start and that I like to recommend to anyone just starting out; these are Mac & Cheese (page 84), Fried "Fish" with Tartar Sauce (page 127), Traditional Lasagna (page 111), and Vegan Chili (page 138).

One thing to think about is that a lot of times when people think they're missing a certain food, a big part of what they're craving is actually the seasonings. If you and your family are used to a lot of Old Bay seasoning on shrimp or poultry seasoning on baked chicken, use those in your vegan cooking.

Cooking from the Spirit: How to Use This Book

You may have picked up this book expecting to see something that isn't here. I'm talking about measurements in the recipes. Well, honey, that's because I don't cook from a recipe, and I don't measure anything. I just add what I like, and I do it until my spirit tells me to stop. I always tell people, "You cook how you want to cook." I'll give you the ingredients I generally use to make the dishes in this book, but you have to bring trust—in yourself. You don't need me to tell you the measurements—you got this!

So yes, this is a cookbook, but it's really more of a *guide*. I want you to trust yourself. I want you to know that you don't need a recipe every time you cook. Right? You can trust yourself enough to look at the food in this book and get inspired. And sometimes you might want to use exactly the ingredients I suggest on one of these pages if that's your business. But I also want you to get into the habit of saying, "You know what? I know what I like to eat. I can pull something together and go by my taste buds and my spirit and make magic happen in my kitchen." I am nobody's chef. I'm a wife and a mother who loves really good food. I cook simply every day, just like in this book. Anyone can do it. You can do it.

And you know how people sometimes say veganism is constricting? I think that comes more from thinking that you have to follow strict recipes. That makes us think there must be "rules" to follow, and that if we don't follow them, we'll make a mistake and ruin the meal. Honey, you'll hear me say it over and over again: There is no right or wrong in my kitchen, and I wish the same for you. This method is easy to adapt whether you're making a meal for one or four or eight people. It's completely flexible.

Here's the most important thing: *Taste and season as you go.* When you cook from this book, you're going to primarily be cooking plants, so you don't have to worry much about eating something raw or undercooked that's going to make you sick. Layer up your seasoning; add it all along the way. Ask yourself what it needs. Build your flavor up as you go. And trust yourself. There aren't any rules here, either, but see page xvii for my tips on which seasonings you might want to use in smaller quantities at first, just until you're familiar with them.

One thing you'll see is that I don't use much salt. This is because my family has a history of hypertension going way back. My spice cabinet is full of salt-free and low-salt seasonings. The luxury of not using salt is that you can season as much as you want. And honey, spice is what makes everything right, right? So go ahead and taste everything as you go! There's really nothing here you can't tweak along the way. And for anything else, it's like my granny always said: If you need a lil more flavor once you're done, there's salt and pepper on the table for a reason!

Don't be hard on yourself—just be creative. You got this!

Most times if you just follow your spirit and go into that kitchen and have some fun and think about the things you love the taste of and pull some things together, you'll make some magic happen. And don't take yourself so serious. Don't overthink it. Let it just come together. That's literally how I cook, and it's the best way to me. You know? That's exactly why we cook from the spirit.

We're *all* capable of doing that if we trust ourselves. So think of this book as an opportunity to trust *you* just a little bit more. Have fun with this moment. You deserve that.

Have fun and enjoy. I love you.

Now, let's go on and get to cooking from the spirit. Yes? Very good!

TAB'S KITCHEN TIPS

- I clean vegetables the way my granny taught me: Use a mixture of warm water, salt or sugar, and a little bit of apple cider vinegar. The salt or sugar helps get any dirt off and the vinegar helps get them squeaky clean.

- Buy on sale! I shop at every sort of store—regular grocery, Asian markets, dollar stores, general merchandise stores, farmers' markets, and flea markets; if they sell food, I'll shop there. Especially if their prices are good! For nonperishables and frozen foods, I'll buy a little extra when the price is low and save it for a meal the next week. Or the next month, because that's my business.

- Do whatever you got to do to not waste food! When your refrigerator is full of fruit and vegetables, you come up with creative stuff. Roast them, make a soup, pull out some flatbreads or bagels or mushroom caps and make some pizza, or use them to stuff peppers or squash. This book is full of ideas for you.

- After you've eaten your last pickle out of the pickle jar, save the jar and the juice. Add cut-up veggies to it and let them sit in the fridge for a day or a week. You can add peppers, sliced onions, peeled garlic, okra—pretty much anything can go in there! Add mushroom caps and later you can use them to make Vegan Deviled Eggs (see page 72). Try adding avocado halves (with the pit still in or not and the skin still on)—they'll change your life, honey.

- Boiling pasta and grains in vegetable broth with some herbs gives them more flavor.

- We eat with our eyes, so keep your food bright. The color's gotta match the flavor! Add your greens last to keep them beautiful.

- Some cravings don't go away, and that's okay! I love seafood. I mean it. I really, really love it. But I haven't eaten it in years, and I don't intend on eating it ever again. That doesn't mean I don't still love it, but there are lots of other things that I can eat instead. You'll find lots of ideas here for dishes that I made vegan because I missed them so much the old way.

- When fighting inflammation, don't use too much oil—use vegetable broth or water instead. Garlic is also really good for inflammation.

- Listen to your body! Some people say nightshades like tomatoes and peppers can cause pain. These are great inflammation-fighting foods, so if you don't have a sensitivity to them, eat up! We all have sensitivities to different things, so listen to *your* body. It won't lie to you.

PANTRY AND FRIDGE

Here's what's in my pantry, refrigerator, and freezer pretty much all the time.

- Avocado (of course)
- Bell peppers—green, red, orange, and yellow
- Mushrooms of every kind!
- Potatoes—I always have thin-skinned red on hand, and I also love russet, white, purple . . . heck, I love them all!
- Sweet potatoes and yams
- Lemons and limes
- Purple onions—you know, the ones they call "red"
- Garlic—fresh or jarred minced, because it's my business
- Whole wheat bread
- Dave's Killer Bread—sprouted or cinnamon raisin
- Canned young green jackfruit
- Jarred or canned hearts of palm
- Canned or frozen cooked chickpeas
- Jarred or canned tomatoes with garlic
- Dried pasta—spaghetti, linguine, angel hair
- Rice
- Vegetable broth or vegan no-chicken broth
- Better Than Bouillon vegetable bases
- Coconut aminos or liquid aminos—these add a savory flavor to food (you can use soy sauce instead)
- Liquid smoke
- Nutritional yeast
- Cashews

- Pecans
- Chickpea flour or rice flour
- Bone char–free sugar (just like regular sugar, but no animal products are used)
- Extra-virgin olive oil
- Grapeseed oil
- Cashew milk yogurt
- Vegan butter
- Sweet relish
- Yellow mustard
- Vegan mayonnaise
- Dill pickles—most pickles are vegan (my favorite brand happens to be Claussen)
- Foodies Vegan Pumfu (or tofu, if you prefer it)
- Field Roast sausages
- Vegan cheese—I buy whatever's on sale, but I especially like Daiya and Follow Your Heart

SPICE AND DRIED HERB CABINET

As I mentioned earlier, for health reasons, I minimize my salt use. When I do include salt, it's Himalayan pink salt, which is a less-processed and healthier option; you can use less and get all the flavor. Otherwise I rely on a few tried-and-true seasonings to make my cooking delicious. Here's what's in my kitchen cabinet full of spices and dried herbs:

- Garlic powder, *not to be confused with* garlic **salt**—garlic powder is just garlic, so I can add as much as I want without worrying about how much salt I'm adding
- Onion powder
- Salt-free seasonings, with or without garlic:
  Garlic and herb seasoning
  Lawry's seasoned garlic powder with parsley, sunflower oil, and garlic
  Onion and herb seasoning
  Poultry seasoning, for seasoning mushrooms as you would chicken
- Everything bagel seasoning
- Curry powder

When a Little Goes a Long Way

I cook from my spirit, but when it comes to these seasonings and spices, I've learned that it's better if my mind checks my spirit before she gets too carried away.

Liquid smoke adds a heavenly meaty, smoky flavor, but it can overwhelm everything else if too much is added, so start with just a few drops of it.

Just a little **black salt** (kala namak) goes a real long way toward adding a nice eggy flavor, but you just need a little to get there, so begin by adding a pinch.

Curry powder is a mixture of different spices, and the selection and amounts of each spice are up to the producer, so none of these is exactly the same. Until you know how the one in your hand is going to taste in your food, add just a bit. Layer it in there and taste as you go.

I love the aroma and flavor of ground **cinnamon** and **dried ginger**, but I use a light hand with them because they can be overpowering and it's very easy to overdo it.

I use only a little bit of spice mix that has added salt, and that includes some favorites of mine, like **Old Bay, nori komi furikake,** and some **everything bagel** seasonings.

Remember that with all of these, you can always add more to taste, but you can't take it out once it's in there! Don't overthink it, you got this.

- Nori komi furikake seasoning, to add seafood flavor
- Dried parsley, oregano, basil, and dill
- Black salt (also called kala namak), to add an eggy flavor to dishes—a funny thing is that it's pink, not black, with just a few specks of black in it; you only need a little bit, so a jar will last a very long time
- Himalayan pink salt
- Lemon pepper
- Old Bay seasoning
- Kelly's vegan parm toppings, like Lemon Pepper Parm and Roasted Garlic Parm

EQUIPMENT

And last, here are the pieces of equipment that help make cooking simple and fun.

- Air fryer (but if you don't have one yet, just use your oven)
- Food processor, especially a powerful one like a Ninja
- Blender, especially a powerful one like a Vitamix
- Slow cooker
- Juicer

breakfast & brunch

SAUSAGE SCRAMBLE   3

CARROT BACON   5

PUMFU SCRAMBLE   7

SWEET POTATO AVOCADO TOAST   9

SWEET POTATO HASH   11

HASH BROWNS   12

CHEESE GRITS WITH SAUSAGE   13

RAW "EGG AND BACON" BREAKFAST BURRITO   14

SWEET POTATO PANCAKES   16

OATMEAL-BANANA-PECAN PANCAKES   17

Okay, so they say breakfast is the most important meal of the day. Maybe it is, and if that's true, then what is *most* important is that it tastes good. You can't have one without the other, right? So let's get into some good breakfast ideas that are tasty and fulfilling and let us be creative in the kitchen. And by the way, you can eat these a little later than breakfast. Like for brunch, or dinner, because that's your business.

Sausage Scramble

Believe it or not, Field Roast Apple & Maple sausage was my second video recipe that went viral. And it was my very first time having that sausage! I just could not believe how good it was. I hadn't eaten pork or beef sausage in twenty-plus years because I stopped eating those meats at age fifteen. But prior to going vegan, I loved turkey sausage, so I was craving some sausage. I saw these Field Roast sausages in the grocery store and brought them home and did the thing I do when I'm not sure whether I'm gonna like something: add a whole bunch of veggies to it. That way, even if the thing I'm tasting ain't great, the veggies make it better, good enough that I can still eat it, so nothing goes to waste. I told myself, "Even if it's bad, girl, you're gonna eat it." But honey, I sliced that sausage up and sautéed it, and it was so good. I said, "Oh Lord, I have to do a video and tell people that I found the best sausage of my life."

And my sausage scramble became such a hit. I mean, it literally went crazy viral. And I became a brand ambassador for the Field Roast company because of that video! And after that, I started putting Field Roast sausages in so many different things, they became a staple in my house. But this first dish has a very special meaning to me, and honey, this is very good eating. (Photo on page 4.)

INGREDIENTS

Grapeseed oil

Vegan sausage, such as Field Roast Apple & Maple, sliced

Fresh shiitake or regular white mushrooms, stems removed, caps torn or coarsely chopped

Garlic powder

Chopped orange bell pepper

Sliced black olives (optional)

A few handfuls of baby spinach

FOR SERVING

Hummus

Sliced avocado

Sriracha

INSTRUCTIONS

HEAT a little grapeseed oil in a large skillet over medium-high heat. Add the sliced sausage and mushrooms. Sprinkle some garlic powder on top and cook, stirring, to get a little sizzle going.

ADD the bell pepper and olives and keep stirring and cooking to brown the sausage on both sides.

ADD the spinach and some more garlic powder if you want it. Stir that all around until the spinach wilts. Now you'll see that the big amount of spinach you added goes down to a small amount. It's all right—that's just how spinach do.

SEASON to your own taste, then transfer your scramble to a bowl. Put some hummus and sliced avocado on the side. Drizzle some sriracha—a lot or a little—on top of whatever you want it on top of. Add your fork and get into it.

Tabism: *Be intentional about having an amazing day today!*

Carrot
Bacon,
5

Sausage
Scramble,
3

Carrot Bacon

A while back I was traveling quite a bit and trying lots of different vegan food, and somewhere along the way I tasted a "bacon" made from coconut and another from zucchini. I started wondering if I could do it with carrots, since I'd already made carrot hot dogs (you can try those on page 48). The very first time I tried it, I was like, "Oh no, Tab, let me put a little extra of this or a little bit of that." But honey, when I figured that thing out, and especially when I put it in my air fryer, Lord, have mercy. Don't worry if you don't have an air fryer; you can cook it in the oven, too. That crunch! And it's so full of flavor. And of course it's good for us—it's a carrot! My husband and daughter love it on a BLT . . . or a *CLT*. I also use it in wraps and regular sandwiches, and sometimes I just eat it by itself because that's my business.

INGREDIENTS

Carrots

Coconut aminos, liquid aminos, or soy sauce

Pure maple syrup

Just a dash of liquid smoke, preferably hickory

Garlic powder

Onion powder

Smoked paprika

INSTRUCTIONS

PREHEAT your air fryer to 380°F or your oven to 400°F. If you're using the oven, line a sheet pan with aluminum foil or parchment paper.

USE a vegetable peeler to peel your carrots, then use it to shave the carrots into thin slices. Honey, you just hold it steady in one hand and run that peeler all the way down the length of the carrot to shave off one thin slice at a time.

IN a big bowl, mix some coconut aminos (how much depends on how many carrots you have; you want it to be at least enough to coat the slices, or more if you want to add lots of flavor), a little bit of maple syrup, a dash of liquid smoke, garlic powder, onion powder, and paprika. Stir it up to blend.

PLACE the carrot strips in the mixture and turn to coat. Let them soak for about 2 minutes, or longer if you have time and want more flavor.

IF you're using an air fryer, transfer the strips right on into the basket and cook for 5 to 7 minutes, until they're lightly browned and crispy.

OR lay the strips on the lined sheet pan and roast in the oven, honey, for 10 to 12 minutes, until lightly browned.

Tabism: *Let your spirit guide you.*

Pumfu Scramble

I used to love scrambled eggs and scrambled egg whites. When I first went vegan, I switched the eggs out for tofu until I realized maybe eight months or a year into my journey that I would get headaches after eating that tofu. I had an allergy test that showed I have a progressive allergy to soy. I was devastated. I said, "Oh my God, how am I gonna have my breakfast scrambles that I've grown to love?" And then one day, someone from Foodies, the company that created Pumfu, reached out to me because they saw that I had talked about my allergy to soy and how I couldn't have tofu anymore. This person told me that they make a tofu alternative using pumpkin seeds. I was like, "Say what now?" So they sent me some, and honey, there is just one ingredient, pumpkin seeds, which they process to taste exactly like tofu. It's full of protein, and it's so good, and I love it. I could make my breakfast scrambles again! And that's how the Pumfu scramble came to be.

It's so much fun to find out little things like that. Who ever thought that you could use a pumpkin seed to create a tofu alternative? It blows my mind.

You can eat your scramble just the way it is, or you can put it in a wrap and roll it up into a breakfast burrito. Or if you have some leftover baked sweet potato or squash, you can warm it up and put the scramble right on top of that.

INGREDIENTS

Grapeseed oil

Chopped mushrooms (*you use any kind you like*)

Chopped red bell pepper

Chopped shallot or onion

Chopped garlic

Pumfu (*or tofu if that's your business*)

Salt-free garlic and herb seasoning (*I like McCormick*), or whatever seasoning you like

Kale, stems and ribs removed, leaves chopped

FOR SERVING

Sliced avocado

Kelly's Gourmet Cheezy Parm or other seasoning

INSTRUCTIONS

POUR just enough oil into a skillet to coat the bottom and heat over medium heat. Stir in the mushrooms, bell pepper, shallot, and garlic.

CRUMBLE the Pumfu on top and sprinkle with as much salt-free seasoning as you want to, because that's your business. Sauté for a few minutes to soften the peppers and shallots.

STIR in the kale and cook until it is wilted, about another minute or so.

PUT your scramble on a plate, top with avocado and parm, and enjoy!

Tabism: *If it's meant to be, it will be, so don't allow yourself to spend time worrying about things you can't control.*

Sweet Potato Avocado Toast

I love avocado so much, I could put it on pretty much anything. And I love sweet potatoes almost as much as I love avocado. One day I was wondering how they would taste together. And then I thought, *If I slice the sweet potato thin, I can use that as toast.* Because you know sweet potato is a healthier option than bread. So now sweet potato avocado toast is one of my favorite things, because it's made from two of my favorites, and because it's sweet, savory, and delicious.

INGREDIENTS

Sweet potato, scrubbed

Sliced avocado

Sliced tomato

Pepitas (pumpkin seeds)

Everything bagel seasoning* (*I like McCormick*)

Kelly's Lemon Pepper Parm or other seasoning

Fresh lime juice

Pico de Gallo (page 60), for serving, if you'd like

Remember—when using any seasoning that contains salt, don't be heavy-handed!

INSTRUCTIONS

YOU can use a toaster oven or regular oven for these. If you're going to use the regular oven, preheat it to 350°F.

FILL a pot that's just big enough to hold your sweet potato(es) with enough water to cover the sweet potato by about an inch. Bring the water to a boil over medium-high heat.

ADD the sweet potato and boil for about 5 minutes so it softens just a little bit. Remove the pot from the heat and let the sweet potato sit in the water for another 5 minutes or so—you want it a little soft, but not too soft.

TAKE the sweet potato out of the water and cut it lengthwise into slices that resemble a slice of bread.

SET a toaster oven to 350°F and toast the slices for about 6 minutes. (If you're using the oven, put the slices on a sheet pan and toast them in the oven for 10 to 15 minutes.) Poke one side of the slices all over with a fork to make sure they're cooked enough and to let some of whatever you're putting on top spread on down into the sweet potato. If the slices are not soft enough, toast or bake again for a few minutes until they are.

PLACE some avocado slices on top of each sweet potato slice, smooshing them down with a fork a little if you want to. Add some tomato slices, pumpkin seeds, everything bagel seasoning, lemon pepper parm, and a sprinkle of lime juice. And of course you can always top it with a little pico de gallo or something like that, if you'd like. Eat with a fork or right out of your hand. Yes, Lord.

Tabism: *Today, add avocado to one of your meals. You can even throw it in a smoothie.*

Sweet
Potato
Hash,
11

Hash
Browns,
12

Sweet Potato Hash

Listen, I love hash browns, and I got my love of any kind of potato from Moma. But of course we know that white potatoes maybe aren't the best for eating every day. Sweet potatoes (or, you know, yams, like we call them sometimes) are the healthy potatoes, as they say, and they are so good and so flavorful. I love a sweet and savory mix, so I decided one day to make a *sweet potato* hash, for a healthier option, but also for something delicious, honey. Plus, I just love bright and vibrant food. We eat first with our eyes, and sweet potatoes bring the color to your plate.

Hash made with sweet potatoes also helps me to not feel so heavy, like I feel sometimes when I eat regular hash. You know, the sweet potato has got a little extra fiber and things in there, so it don't stay long, if you understand what I'm saying. It's really, really good and it also makes you feel good both in your body and about what you're eating. That's why I love it!

INGREDIENTS

Sweet potatoes, cut into large chunks (*I scrub them and leave the skin on. You may not, but I do because that's my business*)

Grapeseed oil

Garlic powder

Dried cilantro (*if you like it. If you don't like it, honey, do it your way!*)

Sea salt

Ground black pepper

Chopped bell pepper (*green, red, yellow, any colors you like*)

Chopped fresh spinach leaves

FOR SERVING

Sliced avocado

Salsa

Kelly's Lemon Pepper Parm

INSTRUCTIONS

PUT the sweet potato pieces into a food processor and process to chop them up small (⅛- to ¼-inch pieces).

HEAT a little grapeseed oil in a large skillet over medium heat and add the chopped sweet potatoes. Add some garlic powder, cilantro, salt, and black pepper and stir to mix it up. Cook for a little bit, until the sweet potato starts to soften.

COVER the pan, because that helps the sweet potatoes get soft, and cook for about 2 minutes.

NOW add your chopped bell pepper and spinach and stir to mix it all together. Cook for another minute or so.

SPOON your sweet potato hash on a plate and top it with avocado, salsa, and a little lemon pepper parm.

DIG in! When you eat this, can't nobody get on your nerves for the whole day long!

Tabism: Get in that mirror and repeat after me (use my voice, if you need to): "Honey, you did that!! I'm so proud of you, I love you, and you are in control, so you can do anything you desire to better yourself and your situation!"

Hash Browns

Hash browns are a Southern breakfast staple. When I was growing up, there was always hash browns with breakfast, whether we were going out to eat or going to my grandma's house. My mama was a big fan of potatoes. Moma used to say that she always gave up potatoes for Lent because she felt like she had such an addiction to them that it had to be sinful. But during the rest of the year, she taught me a lot about potatoes and how amazing they are. Hash browns, baked potatoes, potato chips, french fries, creamed potatoes—any and all of those things are delicious. So why not start your day off right, with potatoes for breakfast? These will give you all the good crispiness when made using an air fryer; you can use your regular oven if that's what you have, and that's your business. (Photo on page 10.)

INGREDIENTS

Russet potatoes, peeled or unpeeled (*depending on how you like them*), cut into large chunks

A few slices of white onion

Garlic powder

Onion powder

Ground black pepper

Sea salt

Grapeseed oil

Ketchup or another favorite condiment, for serving

INSTRUCTIONS

PREHEAT your air fryer to 400°F or your oven to 425°F. If you're using the oven, line a sheet pan with aluminum foil or parchment paper.

PUT your potatoes and onions in a food processor and process to chop them all up into small (⅛- to ¼-inch) pieces. If you don't have a food processor, you can chop them by hand. Transfer the mixture to the air fryer or a large bowl (if you're using your oven).

ADD some garlic powder, onion powder, pepper, a pinch of salt, and a little bit of grapeseed oil and mix to combine. If baking, transfer the mixture to the lined sheet pan.

AIR-FRY for 15 to 18 minutes or bake for 20 to 25 minutes, until cooked through and lightly browned in spots.

SERVE with ketchup, of course, or whatever you like better than ketchup.

Tabism: *You are worthy of happiness, and you deserve to have some fun!*

Cheese Grits with Sausage

I grew up eating grits pretty much just one way—with a little bit of butter and sugar and some cheese in there, the way my mama made them. Yes, I said sugar. After I went vegan, cheese grits were still a favorite of mine—once I figured out my favorite vegan cheeses. And when I want a little bit of savory in there and to make it a little more filling, I'll add some vegan sausage. No matter how I eat them, grits always remind me of home.

INGREDIENTS

Vegan breakfast sausage, like Field Roast Smoked Apple & Sage (*if you want some*)

Grapeseed oil

5-minute or instant grits

Vegan butter

Vegan cheddar cheese shreds

Sugar, or salt and ground black pepper

INSTRUCTIONS

BEFORE you get started making your grits, if you want some sausage in there, go ahead and finely chop that. Heat a little oil in a pan and sauté the sausage just until lightly browned.

FOLLOW the directions on the box to cook up your grits however you want to—in a pot on the stove, or in the microwave if you don't have time for full cooking today.

WHILE the grits are still hot, stir in some butter and some cheese. Add a pinch of sugar or a pinch each of salt and pepper. Stir in your sausage if you made it. You finna eat so good this morning, honey.

Tabism: *Rest, honey. You need it!*

Raw "Egg and Bacon" Breakfast Burrito

I like raw burritos when I'm cleansing or doing raw, because I need to *chew* something! Juices and smoothies can get old, and I can start feeling like I want to chew the air. This is a great option for those moments. When you're not doing raw, you can cook the zucchini in an air fryer or bake it in the oven to change its texture.

INGREDIENTS

Zucchini

Low-salt or salt-free seasoning (*I like to use a smoky one here*)

Garlic powder

Pure maple syrup

A dash of coconut aminos, liquid aminos, or soy sauce, or a few drops of liquid smoke

Thinly sliced fresh or canned (not dried) coconut, drained if canned

Black salt (kala namak; see page xviii)

Ground black pepper

Raw veggie wraps (*I like WrawP brand*) or large bok choy, cabbage, or kale leaves

Guacamole (page 59) or sliced avocado

Pico de Gallo (page 60)

Some leafy greens (optional)

Sliced bell pepper (optional)

INSTRUCTIONS

USE a vegetable peeler to shave the zucchini lengthwise into long, thin strips. Lay the strips in a shallow bowl or on a plate. Sprinkle them with some seasoning and a little bit of garlic powder. Pour a little maple syrup on top. Drizzle on some coconut aminos or add a few drops of liquid smoke. Flip the strips a few times to fully coat them in the marinade. (This is our "bacon.") Set aside.

LAY the coconut in another shallow bowl or plate. Sprinkle on a couple pinches of black salt, followed by a little garlic powder and black pepper. Set aside.

BRUSH or sprinkle a little water on the veggie wrap to soften it and lay it (or your big green leaf) down on a plate or on the counter. Spread some guacamole or a few slices of avocado on the bottom half. Lay a few slices of coconut on top (that's our "egg"), then spoon some pico de gallo on top of that. End with a few slices of zucchini "bacon." If you're using them, add your leafy greens and sliced bell pepper on top.

ROLL the wrap or leaf right up, say yourself a prayer ("OOHHH, GOD, WE THANK YOU"), and eat it up.

Tabism: *Don't allow a bad dream to ruin your day. Release those negative thoughts right now, and know that you and God are in control of your life and all is well!*

Sweet Potato Pancakes

Bringing the aromas and flavors of Thanksgiving to any given morning is a blessing. That's what I feel like when I have sweet potato pancakes for breakfast. Let's go on and get into it.

INGREDIENTS

These amounts are approximate to make about ten 4-inch pancakes, but still trust your spirit as you go . . .

1 cup pancake mix (*make sure it's vegan; some are, even if they aren't specifically labeled "vegan"*)

1 cup plant-based milk, such as coconut or cashew

⅓ cup mashed cooked sweet potato

2 tablespoons shredded coconut

¼ teaspoon ground cinnamon

Grapeseed oil

Pure maple syrup, for serving

INSTRUCTIONS

IN a large bowl, combine the pancake mix, milk, sweet potato, coconut, and cinnamon and whisk or stir until well blended. The mixture should be a little thick but still thin enough to drop off the whisk or spoon.

HEAT some oil in a cast-iron or other heavy skillet over medium heat. Pour a spoonful of the batter into the pan for each pancake; fit as many as you can in there without letting them touch. Let them cook a bit until they get toasty on the bottom.

WHEN the edges are dry and they have several little holes on the surface, it's time to flip them! If they're browning too fast on the bottom for your taste (personally, I love browned and crispy edges), just turn your heat down a little. Unless you like them fluffy, use your spatula to press them down a bit and cook the other side until lightly browned.

ENJOY with maple syrup!

Tabism: *When someone tells you that you can't do something, they are most times saying they can't do it.*

Oatmeal-Banana-Pecan Pancakes

Pecans have been such a big thing in my life since I was a little girl. My granny always had big boxes of pecans. I always remember during the holidays we would use her nutcracker to crack them, and we would sit on the porch and eat them. They have always been a favorite. My granny would put them in German chocolate cake and red velvet cake, and my mama used to do the same thing. And so now when I eat pecans, I just naturally think of good times from my childhood. I love them so much, which is why I use them whenever I can, even for things like my taco meat. Pecans make my heart feel so good.

Chance and I used to always go to Denny's before I was vegan, and they had hearty grain pecan pancakes on the menu that I loved. Of course they use eggs and real butter and all that stuff. After I went vegan, I was like, Oh, honey, I really want some of those pancakes. So I just figured, You know what, let me try to create a recipe myself. And I did, and it's one of my favorites. It's also full of protein and fiber, so it's not just delicious but also a healthier option for you. (Photo on pages 18–19.)

INGREDIENTS

These amounts are approximate to make about eight 4-inch pancakes, but still trust your spirit as you go . . .

1 cup uncooked quick-cooking or rolled oats

¼ cup brown rice flour or your favorite pancake mix (*make sure it's vegan; some are, even if they aren't specifically labeled "vegan"*)

½ cup vanilla almond milk or other plant-based milk

1 to 2 teaspoons raw agave syrup (optional)

½ to 1 banana, mashed

½ to 1 teaspoon ground cinnamon

2 tablespoons or so crushed pecans

Grapeseed oil

Pure maple syrup, for serving

INSTRUCTIONS

IN a large bowl, mix together the oats, flour, milk, agave syrup (if you want it), banana, cinnamon, and pecans. The mixture should be easy to drop from a spoon, but not so runny that it goes all over the place. Trust yourself. If you feel you need a little bit more of something, go with it.

HEAT some oil in a large skillet or sauté pan over medium heat. Pour a spoonful of the batter into the pan for each pancake; fit as many as you can in there without letting them touch. Let them cook a bit until they get toasty on the bottom.

WHEN the edges are dry and they have several little holes on the surface, it's time to flip them! If they're browning too fast on the bottom for your taste (personally, I love browned and crispy edges), just turn your heat down a little. Press them down a bit with your spatula and cook the other side until lightly browned.

ENJOY with maple syrup!

Tabism: *Have coffee or tea today, but add almond or coconut milk to lighten it up! You can even add some agave syrup to sweeten it.*

Oatmeal-Banana-
Pecan Pancakes,
17

pizza & good stuff

FLATBREAD VEGGIE PIZZA WITH PINEAPPLE   25

MEXICAN PIZZA   27

BROCCOLI ALFREDO PIZZA   29

SAUSAGE LOVER'S BAGEL PIZZA   31

PORTOBELLO PIZZAS   33

STUFFED BELL PEPPERS   35

LOADED BAKED WHITE SWEET POTATO   37

STUFFED AVOCADO   39

STUFFED SPAGHETTI SQUASH   41

So here's the thing about pizza.

There ain't no right or wrong way to do this because it's your pizza. You do it your way, that's your business. You can use whatever you got in your refrigerator—if it don't sound crazy to you, go ahead and use it. It can't go wrong. It might make you go more regular, but that's it, and that's a good thing anyway. When it's time to clean out the refrigerator and use veggies before they go bad, throw them babies on a crust, bake it up, and call it pizza night.

Okay, now let's talk about *stuff*. Sometimes stuff in our life is a little bit overwhelming. It can feel heavy on top of us, and it can feel heavy *inside* of us—especially if we respond to it by stuffing ourselves with stuff that isn't good for us.

But stuffing our *food*—instead of stuffing our bodies—well, that's a different story. If I stuff a bell pepper or an avocado with all sorts of good things that are delicious and filling, it will give me good satisfaction.

So let's retrain our minds from thinking . . .

What will we stuff ourselves with to avoid thinking about this heavy stuff inside of us?

. . . to . . .

We don't want or need to stuff our life—or our bodies. We don't want to just keep carrying more stuff on and in ourselves.

Stuffing our food is a great way to retrain our minds. It's actually very therapeutic. And we can layer it with all sorts of good ingredients, so that we're making sure we're not filling ourselves with bad stuff.

Making Pizza Tab's Way

Cover your pan with aluminum foil or parchment paper to help the pizza not stick when the cheese melts.

I use jarred pasta sauce for my pizza because it's just easier to buy one kind of sauce that I can use however I want to—on pasta or pizza or whatever (because that's my business). But you do it how you like it. If you want pizza sauce, you go ahead and use that.

When you're making vegan pizza, you can pile your ingredients on there as high as you want. It's all vegetables (and sometimes fruit). There's no meat, so you're not going to kill anyone if it's not cooked.

I cut my pizza with scissors. I don't understand why everyone doesn't do this.

Flatbread Veggie Pizza with Pineapple

I love pizza, and when I was pregnant with my son, I loved it even more. I loved it so much that I would do a U-turn if I saw a pizza-by-the-slice sign. Then when Quest was maybe about two or three years old, I realized his love for pizza was almost like mine had been. And then one day he asked for pineapple on his pizza, and I got super excited about it because that's something I love, and you know most kids only just want plain cheese. Ever since that day, whenever I make his cheese pizza, I add pineapple. Of course I add tons of veggies to mine as well, but I figure he's getting a little bit of fruit in, even if it happens to be on pizza. I think everybody should try it!

INGREDIENTS

Flatbread (*I use whatever looks good at the store, after I read the label to confirm it's vegan*)

Your favorite vegan pasta sauce or pizza sauce

Vegan mozzarella cheese shreds

Sliced black olives

Sliced white mushrooms

Chopped fresh pineapple or canned pineapple packed in 100% juice, drained very well

Chopped red bell pepper

Sliced purple (red) onion

Fresh baby spinach

Garlic powder

Everything bagel seasoning* (*I like McCormick*)

Sea salt

Remember—when using any seasoning that contains salt, don't be heavy-handed!

INSTRUCTIONS

PREHEAT the oven to 450°F. Line a sheet pan with aluminum foil or parchment paper.

PUT your flatbread on the lined sheet pan and spread some sauce on top. I use a pastry brush because I like a thin layer of sauce, but honey, you put as much as you want because that's your business. If you like a lot of sauce, baby, you can use a spoon and spread more on top; there is no right or wrong. You just relax and have fun.

SPRINKLE a lot of or a little cheese on top. Add your olives, mushrooms, pineapple, bell pepper, purple onion, and spinach, spreading the ingredients all across the surface of your pizza. Sprinkle the garlic powder and everything bagel seasoning on top, then add a few pinches of salt. If you want to, you can add a few more shreds of cheese on top to kind of hold it all together.

BAKE for about 10 minutes, then turn your broiler on high and broil for about 2 minutes to brown the veggies on top.

TAKE it out of the oven carefully—it's hot! (And don't forget what I said about those scissors.)

Tabism: *Sometimes the most important thing to feed is the spirit.*

Mexican Pizza

My first job was at Taco Bell when I was fifteen years old. Mexican pizza was one of the first things I learned to make working there. I'm from a small town, and when I was growing up, Taco Bell was the closest thing we had to a Mexican restaurant. Later I discovered authentic Mexican food, and it became one of my most favorite foods. I still love a good Mexican pizza and enjoy making them at home, and I love that it all started when I was fifteen and working at Taco Bell!

INGREDIENTS

Vegan chorizo crumbles or whole vegan sausages

Grapeseed oil or water

Corn tostadas

Vegan refried beans (*I like salsa-style refried pinto beans from Trader Joe's, but you use what you like*)

Vegan pepper Jack cheese shreds

Sliced green onion, plus more for serving

Sliced black olives

Vegetable oil spray (optional)

FOR SERVING

Vegan sour cream

Chopped tomatoes

Sliced avocado

Taco sauce or salsa

Kelly's Taco Tuesday Parm or other low-salt taco seasoning

INSTRUCTIONS

PREHEAT the oven to 450°F. Line a sheet pan with aluminum foil or parchment paper.

IF your chorizo is in whole links, cut them into pieces and pulse a few times in a food processor to make crumbles.

HEAT a bit of oil or water in a skillet over medium heat and add the chorizo crumbles. Cook for about 5 minutes, stirring once or twice, until the crumbles are heated all the way through (and the water, if you're using it, has all evaporated). Take the pan off the heat.

PUT half your tostadas on the lined sheet pan. Spread some refried beans on the tostadas, then spoon some chorizo crumbles on top.

TOP each one with another tostada and put another layer of beans and then chorizo on top.

SPRINKLE some cheese on top of each one, followed by green onions and black olives. If you want to help your cheese melt a little more, give each pizza a quick spray with vegetable oil. Bake for 10 minutes, or until the cheese is melted.

TRANSFER your pizzas to plates. If you want to, top each one with vegan sour cream, tomatoes, more green onions, and avocado. Drizzle some taco sauce or salsa on top and sprinkle with some taco seasoning. You can eat it whole, right out of your hand, or cut it in half or in quarters.

OOHHH, GOD, WE THANK YOU for this Mexican pizza on Taco Tuesday or any day!

Tabism: *Many are called but few are chosen. Know that there is great power in just being you.*

Broccoli Alfredo Pizza

Before I was vegan, shrimp Alfredo and chicken Alfredo were both favorites of mine. When you take the shrimp and chicken out of the equation, honey, you just got good old broccoli and your sauce. So I add mushrooms to substitute for the shrimp or chicken. Alfredo is just one of those comfort foods that takes me to a time when I thought I was being fancy in the kitchen. Even though I wasn't doing anything super fancy, it felt like I was—like, "Oohhh, I'm making *Alfredo*." Learning how to do that just gave me so much joy and made me feel like I could really *cook*. I still make it for my family, who all love it, too, and that makes me feel very, very good.

INGREDIENTS

Prepared pizza crust

Extra-virgin olive oil

Vegan Alfredo sauce, homemade (see page 119) or store-bought jarred sauce

Marinated artichoke hearts, drained and sliced

Fresh baby spinach

Small broccoli florets

Sun-dried tomatoes packed in oil or softened in water, sliced if large

Sliced or broken-up mushrooms

Thinly sliced red bell pepper

Thinly sliced purple (red) onion

Sliced black olives

Minced garlic

Dried basil

Vegan mozzarella cheese shreds

Kelly's Gourmet Cheezy Parm or other vegan parm, for serving

INSTRUCTIONS

PREHEAT the oven to 400°F. Line a sheet pan with aluminum foil or parchment paper.

PLACE your pizza crust on the lined sheet pan and brush a little olive oil on it. Spread some Alfredo sauce on top.

NOW add whatever you like on top. I like sliced marinated artichoke hearts, a little fresh spinach, broccoli florets (cut them small so they cook), sun-dried tomatoes, some mushrooms, bell peppers, purple onion (except if you're making this for my husband, Chance, or anyone else who doesn't like onions), and black olives.

SPRINKLE a little minced garlic and some dried basil all over the top, and finish with a handful of your vegan mozzarella.

BAKE until the vegetables are tender and the cheese is melted, about 15 minutes. Sprinkle a little more dried basil and some cheesy parm on top before you eat.

Tabism: *Look in the mirror and see your strength! Repeat after me: I made it this far and I am not done!*

Sausage Lover's Bagel Pizza

Being from the South, we didn't really have authentic Italian pizza restaurants. We had Pizza Hut. Growing up we used to get the sausage lover's pizza there, and I loved it. And so when I discovered vegan sausage, I was like, "Oh, honey, I can do this!" It's nice that we vegans can still have a traditional favorite. As for the bagel, you know, it's kind of fun; a good thing about it is that one bagel makes two pizzas! Kids love them and adults do, too, especially when we're trying not to overeat or overindulge. If we put it on a bagel, we just feel a little bit better about it, and that's our business to do so!

INGREDIENTS

Grapeseed oil

Vegan Italian sausage, sliced

Onion bagels, cut in half

Extra-virgin olive oil

Your favorite vegan pasta sauce or pizza sauce

Minced garlic

Vegan mozzarella cheese shreds

Vegan pepper Jack cheese shreds

Baby spinach

Chopped purple (red) onion

Sliced white mushrooms

Diced red and green bell peppers

Sliced black olives

Dried oregano

Torn fresh basil leaves or other herb, for serving

INSTRUCTIONS

PREHEAT the oven to 400°F. Line a sheet pan with aluminum foil or parchment paper.

HEAT some oil in a skillet over medium heat and add your sausage slices. Cook until browned, about 5 minutes. Flip them and cook until the other side is browned, about 5 minutes. Take the pan off the heat.

ARRANGE the bagels cut-side up on the lined sheet pan. Brush with olive oil.

SPREAD the sauce over the bagels, then sprinkle with a bit of garlic. Top with the vegan mozzarella and pepper Jack cheeses.

ADD the sausage slices and any other toppings you like, such as spinach, purple onion, mushrooms, bell peppers, and olives. Sprinkle a little more cheese and dried oregano on top.

BAKE until the cheese is completely melted, about 15 minutes.

Tabism: *When you've got a little less of something than you wish you did, cut it in smaller pieces so it feels like you've got a little more than you do.*

Portobello Pizzas

You know I'm a mushroom lover, and this is a good mushroom lover's pizza, honey, because your crust *is* a mushroom! I use portobello caps as a substitute for regular pizza crust because I love them! But portobello caps are also a good alternative to bread for people who are trying to watch their carbs or who are gluten-intolerant or have a sensitivity to it. If you use portobello caps that are big enough, they even look like bagel pizzas.

INGREDIENTS

Medium red potatoes

Sea salt

Portobello mushroom caps, gills gently scooped out with a spoon

Garlic salt

Salt-free garlic and herb seasoning (*I like McCormick*)

Vegan cheddar cheese shreds or slices (*I like the slices that come in perfect circles*)

Small broccoli florets

FOR SERVING

Salsa

Vegan sour cream

Vegan bacon bits

Sliced avocado (*if you want it*)

INSTRUCTIONS

PUT the potatoes in a saucepan and cover with water by about 2 inches. Add a little salt to the water. Bring the water to a boil over medium heat. Boil until tender but not falling apart when poked with a skewer or sharp knife, about 10 minutes (but the timing depends on what size they are, so keep an eye on them). Drain the potatoes and set aside until cool enough to handle, then slice them crosswise into rounds.

PREHEAT the oven to 350°F. Line a sheet pan with aluminum foil or parchment paper.

SPREAD the portobello caps on the lined sheet pan, gill-side up. Season them with a little bit of garlic salt and as much salt-free seasoning as your spirit tells you to.

LAY the potato slices on the mushroom caps; if they're big potatoes, just one slice will probably be enough, but if they're smaller, you can go ahead and put more than one up on there. Sprinkle a little more seasoning on top.

SPRINKLE some cheese shreds or lay a slice of cheese on top of the potato slices. Put as many broccoli florets as you want on top.

BAKE for 15 to 20 minutes, until the cheese has melted over the edges of the caps. Check them after 12 to 15 minutes, and if the cheese isn't melting very quickly, turn the broiler on for a few minutes to get that cheese melted right.

BEFORE you serve your portobello pizzas, put a spoonful of salsa on top of each, followed by sour cream, vegan bacon bits, and avocado slices (if you want them). Oh, baby, this finna be good!

Tabism: *Grab your invisible umbrella today. If rain should show up in your day, shield yourself and keep it moving. Also, check the weather—if it's calling for rain, grab your real umbrella, too! Love you!*

Stuffed Bell Peppers

When you're using ingredients like mushrooms and spinach, which shrink up quite a bit when they cook, make sure you start with a lot. If you end up with more filling than you have room for in your peppers, save it to make tacos or to stuff something else, like a portobello mushroom cap or a zucchini halved lengthwise and scooped out.

I don't cook the peppers before stuffing them because I like to keep them with a little bit of crunch, and because that's my business.

INGREDIENTS

Extra-virgin olive oil

Red or green bell peppers

Vegan sausage (*I like Field Roast Smoked Apple & Sage for this*), cut into big pieces

Sliced mushrooms

Fresh spinach leaves or baby spinach

A little bit of chopped fresh tomato

Roughly chopped purple (red) onion

Roughly chopped garlic

Vegan cheddar cheese shreds

Sliced black olives

FOR SERVING

Sliced avocado

Pico de Gallo (page 60)

Fresh cilantro

Sea salt

Ground black pepper

INSTRUCTIONS

PREHEAT the oven to 400°F. Lightly oil a baking dish (choose one that's big enough to hold all your peppers; it's okay if they touch each other—that'll help them stay upright).

NOW, you can cut the peppers whichever way you like them for stuffing. If you want them to stand up straight, slice the stem end off. For pepper boats, cut them lengthwise in half. Either way, remove the stem, ribs, and seeds and rinse them out under running water. Shake them dry. Put them peppers in the baking dish, cut-side up (if the standing-up-straight peppers are having trouble standing real straight, you can slice off a very thin bit of their bottoms to flatten them out). Set aside.

PUT the sausage, mushrooms, spinach, tomato, purple onion, and garlic in a food processor or Ninja—don't overfill; you can do this in two or more batches if needed. Process just until the ingredients are chopped and combined. Transfer the mixture to a bowl and repeat to chop the remaining batches if necessary.

ADD a little oil to a skillet and heat it over medium heat. Add the sausage-and-vegetable mixture to the skillet and increase the heat to high. Cook until the sausage is cooked through and the onions are softened, 5 to 10 minutes; the filling won't cook too much more in the oven, so make sure it's where you want it now.

STUFF the filling into the peppers. Sprinkle cheese on top of them. Add some black olives if you want to.

BAKE until the cheese melts, 10 to 15 minutes.

TOP with a few slices of avocado, some fresh pico de gallo, cilantro, and some salt and black pepper.

OOHHH, GOD, WE THANK YOU! Let's eat!!!

Tabism: *Turn on your favorite song and dance! And do it like ain't nobody watching, honey! Go ahead, get it!*

Loaded Baked White Sweet Potato

Honey, I love a white sweet potato! It's like having a regular white potato with just a touch of sweetness. And you can stuff a potato with whatever you want. Sometimes I add steamed broccoli to this mixture, or sauté some onions, mushrooms, and spinach and then sprinkle the stuffed potatoes with vegan lemon pepper parmesan before and after broiling them.

I can usually find white sweet potatoes at Asian markets, and sometimes the regular grocery store has them. You can use Japanese yams in the same way.

INGREDIENTS

White sweet potatoes

Handful of fresh basil leaves

A few handfuls of baby spinach

Chopped garlic

Avocado oil or extra-virgin olive oil

Everything bagel seasoning* (I like McCormick)

Vegan cheddar cheese shreds

FOR SERVING

Avocado slices

Salsa

Vegan sour cream

*Remember—when using any seasoning that contains salt, don't be heavy-handed!

INSTRUCTIONS

PREHEAT the oven to 350°F. Put the white sweet potatoes right on the oven rack and bake for 1 hour, until they're tender when you pierce them with a sharp knife.

WHILE those potatoes are baking, put your basil leaves, spinach, garlic, a little bit of oil, and a little or a whole lot of the seasoning in a mini food chopper (I use my Ninja). Process for a few seconds to chop everything up.

TAKE the baked sweet potatoes out of the oven and set aside. Turn the broiler to high and set a rack 6 inches from the heat source. Line a sheet pan with aluminum foil or parchment paper.

SLICE the sweet potatoes in half the long way. (Hold them with a clean kitchen towel or pot holder if you need to—they might be hot!) Put them on the lined sheet pan, cut-side up, and use a fork to poke and scrape the cooked potato flesh all the way down the length of each one; you want to break it up a bit so it's ready and willing to accept your spinach-and-basil filling.

SPREAD the filling on top of the cut sweet potatoes; if you want to, reserve a little of that filling to put on top in just a minute.

NOW sprinkle some cheddar all over the filling, then add that reserved filling on top of the cheese. What? You forgot to save some filling to add here? Well, honey, that's just fine.

BROIL the stuffed potatoes until they're heated through and the cheese has melted, 5 to 6 minutes. I like to leave mine in a little longer so the edges of the cheese shreds get a little crispy, but you broil them as long as you like.

NOW, you can eat these just as is, or you can do one of my favorite things: Top each potato half with some slices of avocado and a spoonful of salsa. You can go ahead and add some sour cream to that, too, if you want, because that's your business.

Tabism: *Listen to the positive voice inside, even if it's tiny.*

No-Cook Stuffed
Avocado *top* and
Stuffed Avocado
bottom

Stuffed Avocado

Honey, if you want to get fancy for your friends and family for breakfast or brunch, this is your recipe! It's also delicious and fun to eat but doesn't make a lot of dirty dishes.

INGREDIENTS

Grapeseed oil

Vegan breakfast sausage links, sliced

Fresh shiitake mushrooms, stems removed, caps sliced

Chopped sweet onion

Chopped green bell pepper

Chopped fresh or defrosted frozen peaches (*What's that, you say? You don't like peaches with peppers and sausage? Well, all right, then leave them out.*)

Garlic powder

Salt-free multi-spice seasoning

Chopped fresh spinach or baby spinach leaves

Whole avocados

Kelly's Roasted Garlic Parm or other low-salt seasoning

Sriracha, for serving

INSTRUCTIONS

HEAT a little oil in a skillet over medium heat. Add the sausage, mushrooms, onion, bell pepper, and peaches. Add some garlic powder and multi-spice seasoning and cook, stirring, until the vegetables are softened, about 5 minutes.

ADD the spinach and cook for another 2 minutes, until the leaves are wilted. Take the pan off the heat.

CUT an avocado in half and remove the pit. Scoop all the avocado flesh out of the skin from each half and save those skins. Try not to tear the skins—remember, we're stuffing them with what we're making here. But if you tore them, just serve the filling in a bowl.

DICE up the avocado and put it in a bowl. Add the sausage mixture from the pan and gently stir it all up together.

STUFF the filling back into your avocado skins. Sprinkle with some garlic parm and top with sriracha. OOHHH, GOD, WE THANK YOU!

No-Cook Stuffed Avocado

If you don't want to turn your stove on, enjoy this raw version—aka fancy guacamole—for breakfast or lunch, or as a snack!

INGREDIENTS

Whole avocados

Fresh lime or lemon juice

Chopped tomato

Chopped purple (red) onion

Chopped green bell pepper

Chopped mango

Chopped fresh cilantro, plus more for garnish

Sea salt

Ground black pepper

INSTRUCTIONS

SCOOP out a couple avocado halves, saving the skins and dicing the flesh like I say above. Put the diced avocado in a bowl.

ADD some lime or lemon juice, tomato, onion, bell pepper, mango, and cilantro. Season with some sea salt and black pepper. Mix it all together.

STUFF the filling back into the avocado skins and enjoy!

Tabism: *Look how far you've come! Take a moment and give thanks!*

Stuffed Spaghetti Squash

Spaghetti squash is the perfect example of the old adage "Don't judge a book by its cover." It literally goes from looking like a melon on the outside to having "noodles" on the inside. It's pretty magical, and it's very good! So let's get into this magic!

INGREDIENTS

Spaghetti squash

Grapeseed oil

Garlic powder

Dried herbs (*whatever kind you like*)

Chopped vegan sausage

Chopped green and red bell peppers

Sliced white mushrooms

Chopped onion

Salt-free seasoning

Spinach

Vegan marinara sauce

Vegan cheese shreds (*pepper Jack, mozzarella, whatever you like*)

FOR SERVING

Chopped fresh cilantro

Kelly's Gourmet Cheezy Parm

INSTRUCTIONS

PREHEAT the oven to 350°F. Line a sheet pan with aluminum foil or parchment paper.

RINSE the squash and slice it the long way down the middle to cut it in half. Use a spoon to scoop out and discard the seeds from both halves. Rub grapeseed oil on the cut and scooped parts, then sprinkle with garlic powder and your favorite herbs.

PUT the squash halves on the lined sheet pan, cut-side down. Bake the squash until the flesh is tender (you can poke the squash with a skewer or sharp knife to tell) and the edges are browning, 45 minutes to 1 hour.

WHILE the squash is baking, heat a little bit of oil in a skillet over medium heat. Add the sausage and sprinkle with some garlic powder. Cook until firm and beginning to brown.

ADD the vegetables to the pan one at a time, starting with the firmest (if you're using the vegetables listed above, start with the bell peppers). Cook each vegetable until it starts to become tender, then add the next one. Season with garlic powder and salt-free seasoning as you go. Add the spinach last and take the pan off the heat as soon as it's wilted, 30 seconds to 1 minute. Add a few spoonfuls of marinara sauce (just enough to moisten the vegetables), and stir it around to incorporate and warm the sauce.

TAKE your squash out of the oven and increase the oven temperature to 450°F.

TURN the squash cut-side up on the lined sheet pan and stuff the filling into the scooped-out part of each half. Top with cheese. Bake until the cheese melts, about 10 minutes.

TOP with a little cilantro and parm and serve. Tell people that when they eat it, they can run their fork through the squash to make squash noodles. Enjoy!

Tabism: *Remember, today is a different day and another chance to get it right!*

burgers, sandwiches & tacos

Sometimes food and life are like mirrors of each other, aren't they? For instance, when I consider this chapter, I think about how burgers, sandwiches, and tacos are all made up of *layers*. Whatever it is inside each of them, it's all stacked up in there. And a really good sandwich will have layers of ingredients that complement each other so that every single bite tastes delicious.

That's like life, made up of different layers of events and emotions. We want to make sure we apply the same philosophy to our life that we do to our food: layer it up however it will best serve us. If those layers don't balance and match up with each other, things can feel disjointed and out of sync. But when they all come together, and it's just right, things feel very good, maybe even like a nice, warm hug—that's another thing the food in this chapter reminds me of!

OOHHH, GOD, I THANK YOU for burgers, sandwiches, tacos, life, and hugs!

Cheeseburgers, 46

Cheeseburgers

Cooked or canned black beans, well drained and rinsed

Roughly chopped red and green bell peppers

Roughly chopped purple (red) onion

Baby spinach

Roughly chopped portobello mushroom caps (gills gently scooped out with a spoon before chopping)

A few sun-dried tomatoes packed in oil, drained

Garlic powder

Salt-free multi-spice seasoning

Coconut aminos, liquid aminos, or soy sauce

A few drops of liquid smoke

Sea salt

Ground black pepper

Brown rice flour or other gluten-free flour

Vegan cheese slices (I like Violife cheddar slices)

Grapeseed oil (for stovetop cooking only)

When I was a little girl in Eden, North Carolina, my granddaddy used to pick me up after school and take me to this little place called Sealtest. We would get cheeseburgers or hot dogs, depending on our spirits. Oh my God, it was so good. Those were the days. I think that memories are attached to food, and sometimes those memories are what makes something even more delicious and satisfying. That's what cheeseburgers do for me. But if I didn't have that memory, I would still love a cheeseburger. When I was no longer eating red meat but before I became vegan, I still loved turkey cheeseburgers. And when I went vegan, I was like, honey, I got to be able to have a good old cheeseburger.

I like that they can be done in different ways. You can cook them in the air fryer or on the stove, or you can grill them (I usually use a store-bought meat substitute like Beyond or Impossible for grilled burgers). When you're watching your carbs, you can wrap them in lettuce. But most times, I just want that good old bread bun under my burger, and I let that cheese melt right down on it.

When you bite into a cheeseburger, the worries of the world seem to disappear; it just gives a kind of comfort. I think we all deserve to feel that way as often as we can. And I know we all deserve a cheeseburger sometimes. (Photo on page 45.)

INSTRUCTIONS

PREHEAT an air fryer to 300°F. (If you don't have one, don't worry—you can cook these in a skillet. More on that in a minute.)

IN a high-powered blender or food processor, combine the beans, bell peppers, purple onion, spinach, mushrooms, sun-dried tomatoes, garlic powder, multi-spice seasoning, coconut aminos, a couple drops of liquid smoke, and salt and black pepper. Don't overfill the blender—do this in batches if necessary. Blend or process just until combined and chopped up but not chopped so fine that it's mush. Leave a little texture in there.

TRANSFER the mixture to a large bowl and repeat with your remaining batches, if necessary. Taste a bit of the mixture and add whatever you think it needs.

FOR SERVING

Hamburger buns

Toppings, such as sliced purple (red) onion, sliced tomato, sliced pickles, and baby spinach

Condiments, like ketchup, mustard, and vegan mayonnaise

PRESS together a bit of the mixture to make sure it's moist enough to hold together. If it's very dry, chop some more beans in the blender or food processor or mash them with a fork and add them to the mixture.

ADD a small handful of flour and use your hands to mix it in, then shape the mixture into burger patties. If it's too moist to hold a patty shape, add a little more flour until it's right. Don't add too much flour all at once or your mix might get too dry.

AS you form the patties, put them on the cooking plate of an air fryer. (If they don't fit all at once, cook in batches.) Put the cooking plate in the air fryer and air-fry until the patties are lightly browned and firm, about 12 minutes. Turn off the air fryer.

PLACE a slice of cheese on top of each burger, close up the fryer, and let the heat melt the cheese (but not while the fryer is still on because, honey, it will blow the cheese off; trust me, I know).

IF you don't have an air fryer, heat some grapeseed oil in a large nonstick skillet with a lid. Add the patties and cook until golden brown on the bottom, 3 to 5 minutes. Flip them and cook until brown on the other side, another 3 to 5 minutes. A minute or two before the burgers are done, place a slice of cheese on top of each one and cover the skillet for the final minute or two of cooking (covering the pan helps the cheese melt).

IF you want to, while you're waiting for the burgers to cook, you can toast the hamburger buns. But only if you want to.

PUT those finished cheeseburgers on the bun bottoms but leave the tops off so folks can top their burgers however they want with onion, tomato, pickles, spinach, ketchup, mustard, mayonnaise, and whatever else your spirit moves you to put out.

Tabism: *Today, eat your favorite comfort food!*

Chili Carrot Dogs

Hot dogs are wrapped up in so many memories for me. My mama's second favorite thing to eat after potatoes was a hot dog loaded with chili and coleslaw and onion, the way we eat it in the South. There were those after-school trips to Sealtest with my grandaddy (see page 46) where we'd get hot dogs if we weren't feeling like having cheeseburgers. And also around that time when I was a little girl, my best friend Toye and I used to go with her uncle to the furniture market in High Point, North Carolina, where we'd sell hot dogs to the shoppers. Later, when I was a teenager, my friends and I would go to this convenience store called Times Turnaround where for one dollar you could get two hot dogs (sometimes three, when they were doing a special). You know, we didn't have a lot of money, so we'd get them fully loaded with chili and onions and mustard and relish and a bag of chips, and that would be the meal. And honey, life was just so simple and amazing.

So when I went vegan, I knew I had to find my new loaded hot dog, and I was telling myself that I gotta get this right, because I *need* it. But I was trying not to eat so much processed food, so the store-bought hot dogs weren't an option. Then people started asking me over and over if I'd seen online where you could turn a carrot into a hot dog. And it was one of only a handful of recipes that I ever got online, and of course I didn't follow the recipe exactly, honey. I made it my own. The natural next step was adding my pecan chili.

And that's what I did, and baby, it's so good. Oh my gosh. And it's literally just vegetables. Now, if my mother ever saw this, I know she would laugh and say, "Girl, no you ain't makin' no hot dog outta no carrot!" That makes me smile, just like so many of my memories from when I was a child and teenager. And sometimes that's what I think about when I have my chili dog, you know? Life can be simple and still so amazing. So enjoy that. (Photo on pages 50–51.)

INGREDIENTS

About 1 cup coconut aminos, liquid aminos, or soy sauce

Raw agave syrup

A.1. Sauce

Ketchup

Garlic powder

A few drops of liquid smoke

Peeled whole carrots

INSTRUCTIONS

IN a large Dutch oven or other pot (with a tight-fitting lid) wide enough to hold the carrots lengthwise, combine about 2 cups water and the coconut aminos. Add a few spoonfuls each of agave, A.1., and ketchup, some garlic powder, and a few drops of liquid smoke. Stir it up, then bring to a boil over medium-high heat.

ADD your carrots to the boiling liquid. There should be just enough liquid to cover the carrots; add a bit of water, if necessary. Boil gently until the carrots have softened slightly and the liquid is slightly reduced, 10 to 15 minutes (add more water if necessary to keep the carrots covered). Cover the pot and simmer for about 10 more minutes, until the carrots are tender but still offer a little resistance when poked with a skewer or sharp knife. Use tongs to transfer the carrots to a platter, then pat them dry. Don't clean the

FOR THE CHILI

About 1 pound pecans

Grapeseed oil

Yellow mustard

Raw agave syrup

Ketchup

Chili powder

Salt-free multi-spice seasoning

Garlic powder

FOR THE COLESLAW

Shredded cabbage

Vegan mayonnaise

Vegan honey mustard salad dressing

Garlic powder

Ground black pepper

FOR SERVING

Hot dog buns

Chopped white onion

Condiments like ketchup, yellow mustard, and relish

pot yet—you're going to need that pot and the liquid in it for the chili, so just set it aside.

HEAT a seasoned (or lightly oiled) cast-iron grill pan or skillet over medium-high heat. Brown the carrots on both sides. Transfer to a platter to keep warm.

START your chili: Add 1 to 2 cups water to the liquid left in the pot and bring it to a boil, scraping the bottom and sides of the pot to loosen up any bits stuck there. Stir in the pecans and add more water if necessary so the nuts are covered with liquid. Boil gently, uncovered, for about 15 minutes, until the pecans are softened (add more water if necessary to keep the pecans covered).

MEANWHILE, make the coleslaw: Put the cabbage in a large bowl and add a bit of mayonnaise, honey mustard dressing, garlic powder, and pepper. Stir it up and you've got yourself a quick coleslaw. Taste to see what more seasonings it might need. Set it in the refrigerator until we're serving.

DRAIN the pecans and put them in a food processor. Process on high until chopped fine (the pecans should look like ground beef or turkey, but of course they're not).

HEAT some grapeseed oil in a nonstick skillet over medium heat. Add the ground pecans, mustard, agave, ketchup, chili powder, seasoning, and garlic powder. Stir it up to combine. Cook, stirring, until heated through, 3 to 4 minutes.

BUILD your chili dogs: Put a carrot dog in each bun. Top each with some coleslaw, chili, chopped onions (if you want some), ketchup, mustard, and relish. Now we say a prayer, "OOHHH, GOD, WE THANK YOU," and get on into these chili carrot dogs.

Tabism: Think of a happy time from your childhood! Think of how it made you feel as a child! Today, focus on that childlike happiness and let nothing take it away!

Chili Carrot Dogs,
48

Roast Beefless Cheddar Sandwich

Okay, honey, don't laugh at this. I did not grow up on roast beef and cheddar sandwiches. But in high school, an Arby's opened in our little North Carolina town and I was so intrigued by it, you know? I'd never had it. Somehow I'd heard of their roast beef and cheddar sandwich, and I just remember really clearly going and trying it for the first time. So it wasn't something that I ate a lot of, but like most things, the memory attached to it makes it special.

A little while after I became vegan, I got to thinking about how some people just love a roast beef and cheddar sandwich. Like my sister. She *loves* roast beef, and I do mean real roast beef, okay? And so I just decided one day, let me see if I can make a roast beef–like sandwich using mushrooms. And that's what I did. And it's good. I mean, it's very good.

Now, part of why I did it was hoping my sister would see it and that without any pressure or me telling her, "Girl, you need to do it this way," she might try it out. I don't think she has yet, and that's her business.

INGREDIENTS

Portobello mushroom caps, gills gently scooped out with a spoon

Vegetable broth

Coconut aminos, liquid aminos, or soy sauce

Garlic powder

Onion powder

Dried thyme

Dried basil

Pinch of sea salt

Ground black pepper

FOR THE CHEESE SAUCE

Vegan cheddar cheese shreds

Unsweetened plain cashew milk yogurt

Garlic powder

FOR SERVING

Sweet-and-spicy mustard

Artisan buns or whatever kind of bun you have

INSTRUCTIONS

CUT the mushroom caps from the top into thin slices, like deli meat. Set aside.

IN a large bowl, combine a little broth and a few splashes of coconut aminos (you want enough liquid to coat all the mushroom slices). Add some garlic powder, onion powder, dried thyme, dried basil, salt, and pepper. Stir to combine.

HEAT a dry nonstick skillet over medium heat. Dip the mushroom slices into the marinade, turning them once or twice to make sure they get good and seasoned, and put them in the hot skillet in a single layer. Cook the slices for a minute or two on each side to brown, then remove them from the pan and set aside.

MEANWHILE, make your cheese sauce: In a small saucepan, combine some cheddar shreds, a little bit of yogurt, and a few shakes of garlic powder. Stir over medium-low heat until the cheese has melted and the sauce is well blended, about 5 minutes; remove the pan from the heat.

NOW make your roast beef sandwiches: Put some mustard on the bottom half of the buns, then add some slices of portobello "roast beef," and spoon on a little cheese sauce. Add the top half of the buns and you're ready to eat!

Tabism: *Have yourself a good day. But even if you can't have a good one, don't you dare go messing up no one else's.*

Sloppy Joes

Eating sloppy Joes is a favorite family memory for me. My mama used to make them for us on the nights when we'd all sit down to eat in front of those family shows that we watched together, like *The Fresh Prince of Bel-Air* and *The Cosby Show*. This one is good old comfort food, and it's all from the heart.

INGREDIENTS

1 pound or so vegan ground beef substitute

Garlic powder

Salt-free multi-spice seasoning

Coconut aminos, liquid aminos, or soy sauce

Sugar

Grapeseed oil

Tomato sauce (a 15-ounce can is good for 1 pound of vegan ground beef)

Barbecue sauce

Ketchup

Yellow mustard

Smoked paprika

FOR SERVING

Vegan mayonnaise

Hamburger buns

Dill pickles

INSTRUCTIONS

IN a large bowl, combine the ground beef substitute, garlic powder, multi-spice seasoning, coconut aminos, and a small handful of sugar. Mix it up a little bit.

HEAT a little oil in a large nonstick skillet over medium heat. Add the "beef" mixture along with about half a can of tomato sauce, some barbecue sauce, ketchup, mustard, and smoked paprika. Cook, stirring, until the mixture is well combined and heated through.

TURN the heat down to medium-low and cook until the sauce thickens slightly. If the mixture is too dry, add some more tomato sauce and barbecue sauce to give it the right spoonable consistency—honey, it's called *sloppy* Joes for a reason.

TO serve, spread some mayonnaise (*I like extra mayo, but you do it your way*) on both halves of the hamburger buns, then scoop some sloppy Joe mixture onto the bottom halves of the buns and top with the other half of the buns. Put a sliced dill pickle on that plate if you want to. Now turn on your favorite TV show and get into those Joes!

Tabism: *Call someone you haven't spoken to in a while. Do not text . . . call! Let them know you were thinking of them.*

Philly Cheese*fake* Hoagie

We only had a handful of restaurants in my hometown, and one of them is still there to this day. Elizabeth's Pizza was our little Italian spot where we used to go after football and basketball games to have the absolute best cheesesteak hoagies. A while after I went vegan, I got such a craving for Elizabeth's cheesesteak hoagies! So I made one with the pecan "meat" I use for my tacos. Now, this was before my husband went vegan, and when he tried it and said to me, "Oh my God, bae, this is so good," that's how I knew I'd got it right.

Listen, who don't like a cheesesteak? And if we can do a healthier option using veggies and nuts, but still make it a comfort food, then that's just double the fun, right? I get the craving for them especially during the fall and winter, because my memories lead me back to those times at Elizabeth's Pizza. And I'll say to Chance, "Oohhh, let's turn on the game, and let's eat us a cheesesteak!" But of course you know these days it's my own cheese*fake* hoagie. And it is very good.

INGREDIENTS

Grapeseed oil

Pecan meat (see page 62)

Sliced red and green bell peppers

Sliced mushrooms

Sliced white onion

Garlic powder

Dried oregano

Ground black pepper

A few drops of liquid smoke

Vegan cheese shreds (*I like to use mozzarella*)

FOR SERVING

Vegan mayonnaise

Hoagie rolls

Lettuce

Sliced tomato

INSTRUCTIONS

IN a large nonstick skillet with a tight-fitting lid, heat a little oil over medium heat. Add the pecan meat, bell peppers, mushrooms, and onion. Stir in some garlic powder, oregano, black pepper, and a few drops of liquid smoke. Cover and cook, stirring occasionally, until it's all heated through, about 5 minutes.

REMOVE the lid and cook, stirring, for another minute or two, until the vegetables are slightly browned. Add the cheese and cook, stirring, until it's melted.

TO make the cheese*fake* hoagies, spread a little mayonnaise (or a lot) in the hoagie rolls. Spoon some pecan-and-veggie mixture into them and then tuck some lettuce and tomato in there. You're ready to eat.

Tabism: *Be patient with others today . . . All that rushing gets you too worked up, anyway. Also, remember to be patient with yourself.*

Spinach and Mushroom Quesadilla

Why a spinach and mushroom quesadilla? Because I love spinach. I love mushrooms. I love mozzarella. And a quesadilla of any kind is all right in my book. You know Popeye ate spinach to get strong, so throw it on in there and get strong with your quesadilla!

INGREDIENTS

Grapeseed oil

Sliced white mushrooms

Garlic powder or salt-free garlic and herb seasoning (*I like McCormick*)

Chopped white onion

Chopped red and green bell peppers

Baby spinach

Large tortillas (*whole-grain, gluten-free, spinach, or anything else—it's your quesadilla, your business*)

Vegan pepper Jack cheese shreds

FOR SERVING

Guacamole (recipe follows)

Pico de Gallo (recipe follows)

INSTRUCTIONS

HEAT some oil in a large nonstick skillet over medium heat. Add the mushrooms and a little bit of garlic powder or garlic and herb seasoning and sauté for 2 minutes, until the mushrooms are softened.

ADD the onion and bell peppers and sprinkle on a little more garlic powder or seasoning, then sauté for another minute, until the onion and peppers are softened.

ADD the spinach and sauté all the vegetables together for about 1 minute, until the spinach has wilted. Season to taste and remove the pan from the heat.

HEAT a separate large skillet over medium heat. Lay a tortilla in the pan. Spread some cheese on one half of the tortilla. Sprinkle with some garlic powder or seasoning, if you want to.

SPREAD some sautéed veggies on top of the cheese and top with a little more cheese. Fold the other half of the tortilla over the cheese and vegetables. Cook for a few minutes, until lightly browned on the bottom. Flip and brown the other side (and melt that cheese all the way through).

PUT your quesadilla on a plate and enjoy with guacamole and pico de gallo.

Guacamole

Can I talk to you about avocado for a pair of seconds? In order to have the most perfect guacamole, you can't have a hard avocado. It just don't taste the same because it ain't ready yet. It's too hard. A ripe avocado is a little soft, and that's what you want! That's an avocado that's going to make some amazing guacamole.

Ain't that like life? Sometimes we allow the world to influence us so much that it hardens us. It hardens our hearts. And then we can't make beautiful things happen. Oohhh, but baby, when we soften ourselves just a little bit, soften our hearts, the most beautiful things come about.

I want you to remember not to be so hard on yourself. The world is hard enough. You don't have to be hard on you, too. Okay? So take your time. Be gentle with yourself. And now let's make us some guacamole.

INGREDIENTS

Avocados (*I usually start with 3 or 4 but you use what you got*)

Diced purple (red) onion

Diced Roma (plum) tomato

Finely chopped fresh jalapeño (optional)

Chopped fresh cilantro

Fresh lime juice

Garlic powder

Pinch of sea salt

Ground black pepper

INSTRUCTIONS

CUT your avocados in half, then pit them, peel them, and place them in a large bowl. Add the onion, tomato, jalapeño (if you want it), and cilantro. Mix it up a little, using your spatula or spoon to mash up the avocado as much or as little as you want to.

NOW add your fresh lime juice. I say the more lime, the better, but you add as much as you like. It's *your* food.

ADD a sprinkle (or more) of garlic powder, a pinch of sea salt, and some pepper, according to how you like it. Mix that all up together and you're done! Wasn't that easy? Now let's go find us a taco to put this on, okay?

Pico de Gallo

Pico de gallo is one of my most favorite simple dishes that you can just add to so many great things. It's *always* fresh. Some people will also call it *salsa fresca*, which is "fresh salsa" or something. Because we don't even want to *know* what *pico de gallo* means in Spanish, honey! The translation is "rooster's beak"! I have no idea. I don't think that's our business. Our business is to focus on the freshness of the pico de gallo. Let's get into this pico de gallo. Yes? Very good.

INGREDIENTS

Diced Roma (plum) tomatoes

Diced purple (red) onion

Chopped fresh cilantro

Minced fresh jalapeño

Minced garlic

Fresh lime juice

Pinch of sea salt

Ground black pepper

INSTRUCTIONS

IN a medium bowl, combine the tomatoes, onion, cilantro, jalapeño, garlic, lime juice, salt, and pepper and mix well. Taste and add more of whatever you think it needs. Set aside until you're ready to serve it.

Tabism: *Practice forgiving all day! Today, when folks get to cutting up and working on your nerves, just forgive them and let it go! Don't give it any energy other than forgiveness!*

Raw Cheesy Pecan Tacos

I love my pecan taco meat because you can eat it raw or cooked—it's good both ways. After I went vegan, I discovered that a lot of recipes for vegan or raw tacos use walnuts, but I really love pecans and I wondered about doing them the same way. So I tried it and now it's one of my favorites. And not just mine—I have shared this recipe many times, and so many people love it, too. The mango de gallo on top of the pecan "meat" is just the perfect sweet-and-savory combination. But I also love that it's one of those things that you can have when you're eating raw—like if you're on a cleanse and you're trying to stay away from cooked food for a little bit—and you don't feel like you're missing anything because it has so much flavor and texture.

The black garlic powder in the cheesy sauce adds an extra savory, or umami, flavor to the sauce; just use regular garlic powder if you don't have it.

INGREDIENTS

FOR THE PECAN MEAT

Raw pecans

Chopped cremini or other mushrooms

Chopped red and green bell peppers

Chopped purple (red) onion

Chopped garlic

Coconut aminos, liquid aminos, or soy sauce

A few drops of liquid smoke

Salt-free garlic and herb seasoning (*I like McCormick*)

Low-salt or salt-free taco seasoning

FOR THE CHEESY SAUCE

Raw cashews

Garlic cloves

Nutritional yeast

Fresh lemon juice

Black garlic powder or regular garlic powder

Diced fresh jalapeño (*if you like a little spice*)

INSTRUCTIONS

MAKE the pecan meat: Cover the pecans in warm water and soak for 20 to 30 minutes to soften them.

DRAIN the pecans and put them in a food processor. Add the mushrooms, bell peppers, onion, garlic, coconut aminos, a few drops of liquid smoke, and garlic and herb and taco seasonings. Don't overfill the processor bowl—do this in batches, if necessary. Process on high until well blended. Set aside.

MAKE the cheesy sauce: Place the cashews in a medium bowl and add warm water just to cover. Let soak for about 30 minutes to soften them.

TRANSFER the cashews and their soaking water to a food processor. Add the garlic, nutritional yeast, lemon juice, black garlic powder, and jalapeño (if you want it). Blend it all up until smooth. This cheese sauce is a little thicker because we're using it on tacos, but you can add water if you want it to be thinner. I just like it thick so it holds everything together.

MAKE the mango de gallo: Place the mango in a bowl with the cilantro, onion, bell pepper, lemon juice, lime juice, a little dab of garlic powder (I hadn't seen this done in mango de gallo before, but it's my business), and a sprinkle of sea salt. And if you like a little spice in your life, add the jalapeño. It's your mango de gallo—you do it how you want to. Stir it up and set aside.

FOR THE MANGO DE GALLO

1 mango, peeled, pitted, and chopped

Chopped fresh cilantro

Chopped purple (red) onion

Chopped red bell pepper

Fresh lemon juice

Fresh lime juice

Garlic powder

Sea salt

Diced fresh jalapeño (*if you want it, add it—that's your business*)

FOR SERVING

Large lettuce leaves

Guacamole (page 59)

WHEN you're ready to eat, fill lettuce leaves with the pecan meat. Spoon a little guacamole on top, then a little mango de gallo, then some cheesy sauce. And honey, now you're eating!

Tabism: *Remember, there is no darkness without light! So if you're in a dark place, know that it can't exist without light. Find your light again—you deserve it!*

CLOCKWISE FROM TOP LEFT:
Spicy Caribbean-Style Jackfruit Tacos, 65; Raw Cheesy Pecan Tacos, 62; and Sweet Potato Tacos, 64

Sweet Potato Tacos

Listen, I will take any taco just about any day. And today I'll take this one, filled with sweet potatoes, because honey, who don't love a sweet potato? Especially when it's paired with delicious savory ingredients like purple onion, mushrooms, pico de gallo, and avocado. (Photo on page 63.)

INGREDIENTS

Sweet potatoes, scrubbed and cut into ½-inch dice

Chopped purple (red) onion

Chopped mushrooms

Grapeseed oil

Salt-free multi-spice seasoning

Low-salt or salt-free taco seasoning

Garlic powder

FOR SERVING

Soft or hard taco shells

Pico de Gallo (page 60)

Sliced avocado

Diced purple (red) onion

Chopped fresh cilantro

Minced fresh jalapeño

Fresh lime juice

INSTRUCTIONS

BRING a large pot of water to a boil. Add your diced sweet potatoes and simmer for 5 to 7 minutes. This gets them just soft enough that when we put them in the air fryer, they will cook down and get nice and crispy. Drain the sweet potatoes.

PREHEAT an air fryer to 370°F.

TRANSFER the sweet potatoes to a bowl. Add your chopped onion and mushrooms and mix them in with your potatoes. Add a bit of oil so the seasonings will stick.

ADD the multi-spice seasoning (as much as you'd like, because that's your business), taco seasoning, and garlic powder, then gently mix it all together.

PUT the mixture into the air fryer and let it do its magic for 15 minutes (check it halfway through to make sure it's not sticking and the vegetables are just beginning to brown).

PUT the sweet potatoes in a taco shell and add all the pico de gallo, avocado, purple onion, cilantro, jalapeño, and lime juice you want. Enjoy!

Tabism: *Eat something spicy today, even if it's just one bite!*

Spicy Caribbean-Style Jackfruit Tacos

Oh my goodness, honey, Jack and I are like besties in these tacos, where the jackfruit (that's Jack's full name) is cooked all the way down and is so flavorful and delicious that it does your heart so good. These tacos make you feel like you're somewhere in the Caribbean, just enjoying your vacation and your whole entire life. And you still right there at your house! (Photo on page 63.)

INGREDIENTS

Two 20-ounce cans young green jackfruit packed in brine or water, drained

Grapeseed oil

Salt-free Caribbean seasoning (*I like my Sunshine All Purpose Seasoning from McCormick*)

Salt-free garlic and herb seasoning (*I like McCormick*)

FOR SERVING

Soft or hard taco shells (*or use butter lettuce leaves to make wraps if you're watching the carbs*)

Guacamole (page 59)

Chopped fresh cilantro

Diced tomato

Diced onion

Minced fresh jalapeño (optional)

Salsa or your favorite taco sauce

INSTRUCTIONS

FURTHER drain the liquid out of the jackfruit by squeezing each piece in your hand.

HEAT a bit of oil in a large nonstick skillet over medium heat. Add the jackfruit and the Caribbean and garlic and herb seasonings and sauté until the jackfruit starts to brown and some pieces get a little crispy in texture, 12 to 15 minutes. As the jackfruit cooks and softens, use a spoon or spatula to shred and break it up until it resembles shredded pork or chicken. Turn the heat down if it begins to burn.

USE whichever shell you prefer and load it up with that jack, guacamole, cilantro, tomato, onion, jalapeño (if you want extra spice), and salsa! Say a good lil prayer and honey, go to work!!!

Tabism: *Eat somewhere with a view or eat outside and take in some fresh air.*

Pecan-Cheese Rolls

These fun rolls came from me trying to make taquitos. I mean, they *are* kind of like taquitos, but you can serve them any way you want. They're so good as an appetizer, they're good for a full meal with a little taco salad on the side, and the kids love them. They're convenient, they're quick, they're delicious. And you can add a little heat to them if you want by chopping up a little bit of jalapeño. Or you can leave the heat out of it, if that's your business.

INGREDIENTS

Raw pecans

Kale, stems and ribs removed, leaves roughly chopped

Roughly chopped portobello mushrooms

Roughly chopped red bell peppers

Vegan cheese shreds, such as Daiya cheddar and mozzarella blend

Vegan egg roll wrappers*

Grapeseed oil

Sweet chili sauce, for dipping

*Check the ingredients on the package to make sure your wrappers are vegan—many are not. And don't buy wonton wrappers by accident; they're not as big as egg roll wrappers.

INSTRUCTIONS

PUT the pecans in a large saucepan, add water to cover, and bring to a boil over medium-high heat. Boil for about 10 minutes, until softened.

DRAIN the pecans and transfer them to a food processor. Add the kale, portobellos, bell peppers, and some cheese. Don't overfill the processor—do this in batches if necessary. Process until finely chopped and well combined.

PREHEAT an air fryer to 370°F.

LAY out an egg roll wrapper and put a spoonful of the pecan filling in the center. Add a little cheese. Roll it up, tucking the ends in before you've rolled it all the way up. Wet the loose end of the wrapper to stick it down and seal up your egg roll.

KEEP stuffing and rolling until you run out of filling or wrappers.

BRUSH the filled rolls with a little oil and place in the air fryer. Air-fry until lightly browned and crispy, about 10 minutes.

TRANSFER the rolls to a plate and serve with some sweet chili sauce on the side. You see that melted cheese?? Yes, get into it!

Tabism: *Sometimes our closure is "no closure," and we have to find our peace with it. Stop holding yourself hostage, it's time for your freedom! You are alive—act like it!*

appetizers & sides

You know how before you get started on a goal, you have to do some things that lead up to it? That's how I think about the appetizer before a meal. It's like the little start before you really get started, right? It's a kind of preparation, just a little taste before the main event (whether we're talking about life or food). It's like being told, "Oohhh, things are going to get even better, honey!"

Now, when it comes to side dishes, they are their own version of this. Even when we're on the main thing that we're going through in life, sometimes we got to take a moment and look to the side—to the right, to the left—and sometimes we got to take a little alternate turn. Sometimes, we got to go *over there* for a little bit, and then we can come on back to the main thing. So that's what our sides are—just a little look away from the main course. It's "Let me look over here to see what's going on for a second. Oh, let me taste that. Hmmm, that's good, too." And that little side thing complements the main and brings it all together. You want the main to be enhanced by the little side trip.

And if you want to, as I very often do, you can eat it all at the same time. You can put a little bit of the main on your fork with a little bit of the side, then it all goes down together in one big party. And if you have a little bit of your appetizer left over, you can mix that in the same bite with your main dish and your side dish. Honey, can't nobody tell you nothing; you're doing it all at the same time, and that's your business.

Saved Eggs,
72

Saved Eggs (aka Angel Eggs, aka Vegan Deviled Eggs)

Deviled eggs are a staple in a Southern house. My granny and my mama used to make the best deviled eggs for Sunday dinners and holidays. After I went vegan, for almost four years I didn't have a single deviled egg, and it was one of the things I missed the most. Then one night I had a dream about how I could make a vegan alternative. I even woke up and told people online about how I had dreamed about making the most amazing vegan deviled eggs. I promised I'd let them know how it went, and a day or two later, I posted the video of me making these for the very first time. They were as amazing in real life as they had been in my dream. To this day, I believe that video is one of my most popular recipes, and it shocked so many people, including myself! It was powerful, the way that inspiration struck, and just carried me right on through. I've enjoyed these so many times since then; they're a great way to use the leftover pickle juice whenever I finish a big jar of pickles.

And there's more to these than me reclaiming a dish I've always loved for myself. When I was growing up, I never made deviled eggs because I didn't really like being in the kitchen. But the one thing that my mama used to let me do was sprinkle the paprika on the top. So when I grew up and had a family of my own, of course deviled eggs came with me. And when my daughter was about twelve, sprinkling the paprika on top of the eggs became her job. Soon enough I taught her how to make them, and it became something that we always did together the night before a special day, especially Thanksgiving and Christmas. When we went vegan, we lost that specific shared experience for a few years. I'm so thankful that this idea came to me in a dream so Choyce and I got to share those moments again. And who knows? Maybe that's part of why it came to me in a dream.

Sometimes old memories can be replaced with a new memory, and that's okay. And so now here they are: not my deviled eggs, but my *saved, aka angel,* eggs. I sure do love them. (Photo on page 71.)

INGREDIENTS

Black salt (kala namak; see page xviii)

Juice from a big jar of dill pickles

White mushroom caps (*make it easy on yourself and use good-size mushroom caps with room to fill*), gills gently scooped out with a spoon

Canned chickpeas, drained and rinsed

Vegan mayonnaise

Yellow mustard

Sweet pickle relish

Dried dill

Garlic powder

Pinch of sea salt

Pinch of ground black pepper

Smoked paprika

INSTRUCTIONS

PUT a few pinches of black salt in the pickle juice. Close the jar and shake it up to dissolve the salt. Add the mushroom caps, close the jar, and refrigerate overnight or for up to 1 week. This is to change the texture of the mushrooms to give them the feel and flavor of eggs; trust me, it works! (The longer you leave the mushrooms in the pickle juice, the more pickled they will taste.)

PUT the chickpeas in a food processor and process to chop them up fine. It's okay if there's a little texture in there. If the chickpeas are all hiding under the blade and around the edges of the work bowl, stir in a little vegan mayonnaise or water to get them moving again. Transfer the chickpeas to a medium bowl.

ADD the vegan mayonnaise, yellow mustard (for flavor and color), sweet relish, dill, garlic powder, and a little black salt. Stir it up to blend. Taste and add a pinch of salt and pepper and whatever else you think it needs right now (the black salt gives it that eggy taste, so add more if you want more of that, but remember a little goes a long way). Stir it up again. The texture should be spoonable and not too liquid (like the yolk mixture you use to fill deviled eggs).

REMOVE the mushroom caps from the pickle juice and drain them very well. If they're very wet, you can pat them dry. Put them on a plate.

SPOON some chickpea filling into each mushroom cap. Sprinkle on some smoked paprika. Place in the refrigerator until chilled, then serve. (Or cover them and refrigerate for up to 24 hours before serving.)

Tabism: *You have a dream. It's time to wake up and make it happen, honey!*

Coconut Ceviche

The first time I had ceviche was in 2009. I know what year it was because I was working at a nursing home, and one of my coworkers, Isabel, brought some to work. When I told her I had never heard of ceviche, she explained that it is fish or shellfish marinated in citrus juice so that it firms up as if it were cooked and then mixed with crunchy vegetables. She had made crab ceviche, and she told me I had to try it. Honey, it was one of the best things I had ever tasted in my life. I wrote down everything she told me about how she made hers and I went home and made it for my family using imitation (not vegan) crabmeat. It became one of my favorite things to eat all over Los Angeles, and when we went to Mexico, I knew I had to find ceviche. It is so very good. Then I went vegan, and since Mexican food and seafood are two of my most favorite things, I knew I needed to figure out a way to make myself vegan ceviche. Since then, I've made this dish for so many people, and more than once someone has whispered to me, "Girl, I thought you was vegan??" I am, honey, I am. It's the coconut that tastes so amazing. It's the star of this dish, and all the other ingredients are supporting players (kind of like the avocado is the star of guacamole). (Photo on page 76.)

INGREDIENTS

Canned or jarred coconut meat packed in syrup, drained

Sliced fresh jalapeño

Roughly chopped purple (red) onion

Fresh cilantro leaves

Fresh lime juice

Fresh lemon juice

Nori komi furikake seasoning

Diced fresh tomato

Diced avocado

Garlic powder

Sea salt

Ground black pepper

Tortilla chips, for serving

INSTRUCTIONS

DRAIN the coconut and put it in a food processor. Add some jalapeño, onion, cilantro, lime juice, lemon juice, and nori komi furikake. Process until finely chopped, but don't overblend; you don't want it to turn to mush.

TRANSFER the mixture to a large bowl. Taste and add more of any of the seasonings you think it needs.

ADD the tomato, avocado, garlic powder, and a pinch each of salt and pepper. Stir it together gently. Taste and add more lime juice, salt, or pepper, or anything else you think it needs more of.

TRANSFER your vegan ceviche to a serving bowl and serve with tortilla chips.

Tabism: *Do something you know you need to do, even if it makes you uncomfortable. I believe in you. You got this!*

Mexican Street Corn (*Elote*)

Along with ceviche (see page 74), Mexican street corn, also known as *elote,* is another thing I never had until we moved to Los Angeles. How did I live so long without it? In 2005 my mother came out from North Carolina to visit us. It was the one and only time she actually got to come out to L.A., and I remember it all very well. I took her to The Alley, a downtown shopping area where everything is wholesale and discount. You can get all kinds of great things, and that includes street corn, sold either on the cob or sliced off the cob and served in a little bowl. That day was my very first time having it, so my mama and I got to discover it together. It was so good, and Moma loved it so much. (She loved those street bacon-wrapped hot dogs, too, but that's her business.)

I soon learned how to make a version of street corn at home; over the years I made it lots of times, and when I became vegan, I figured out a new way to make it. Every time I have it, I think of shopping at The Alley downtown with my mom, me pushing her in her wheelchair and her being so excited about eating street corn and then going back to North Carolina and telling everybody at home about it. That's such a pleasant memory, and I'm always happy to spend some time with it. (Photo on page 77.)

INGREDIENTS

Fresh corn on the cob, shucked, rinsed, and dried

Extra-virgin olive oil

Garlic powder

Sea salt

Ground black pepper

Vegan butter (*if you would like it*)

Vegan mayonnaise

Kelly's Gourmet Cheezy Parm or other vegan cheesy seasoning

Chili powder

Dried cilantro or chopped fresh cilantro

Tajín seasoning, *if you're feeling fancy*

INSTRUCTIONS

PREHEAT the oven to 425°F.

PUT the corn in a roasting pan. Drizzle some olive oil on top and sprinkle with garlic powder, a pinch of salt, and some pepper. Roll the corn around to coat it evenly with the oil and seasonings.

ROAST the corn for 20 minutes, then remove the pan from the oven.

IF you'd like to, you can rub the stick of butter on each hot ear of corn, but you don't have to—it'll still be delicious.

BRUSH each ear of corn with mayonnaise and sprinkle all over with the cheesy parm, chili powder, cilantro, and the Tajín (if you're using it). And now you're ready to eat!

Tabism: *Eat something yellow today, and know that the sun shines on you!*

Coconut
Ceviche,
74

Mexican
Street Corn
(Elote), 75

Spicy Tuna Roll

Sushi was something I thought I would have to live without forever after going vegan. It was something my daughter and I shared a love for, and I was sad that we wouldn't have that anymore. Baby, when the Lord placed this spicy tuna roll recipe in my spirit, I knew He loved us a little extra on that day! I make this whenever I juice carrots.

INGREDIENTS

Pulp from juiced carrots (see page 171)

Vegan mayonnaise

Chili-garlic sauce (*I like Huy Fong*)

Nori komi furikake seasoning

Nori sheets (the kind used for sushi)

Sliced avocado

Persian cucumbers, sliced lengthwise into thin wedges

Coconut aminos, liquid aminos, or soy sauce, for serving

INSTRUCTIONS

PLACE the carrot pulp in a medium bowl. Add some vegan mayonnaise, chili-garlic sauce (a little or a lot, based on how spicy you want it), and some nori komi furikake. Stir to combine. The mixture should look like tuna salad; add more mayonnaise, if necessary.

PLACE a nori sheet shiny-side down on a work surface. Use a damp paper towel to pat the sheet and moisten it a bit. (This will make it easier to roll up.)

RUN a mound of spicy "tuna" down the length of the shorter end of the sheet.

TOP with avocado slices and 2 cucumber wedges.

ROLL up tightly and set aside.

REPEAT to make more rolls with the rest of the ingredients.

SLICE the long rolls crosswise into shorter rolls (2 inches long, give or take). Serve with a small dish of coconut or liquid aminos or soy sauce for dipping.

Tabism: *Know your worth and embrace it!*

"Seafood" Salad (aka Crab-less Salad)

My godparents lived in Albany, Georgia, and they were wealthy. When I was a little girl, I would spend a couple of weeks with them each summer. That was where I tasted crab legs and crab salad for the first time. My godmother was a housewife and stay-at-home mom, and cooking very fancy foods was her thing. She just loved to do it. She made her crab salad from scratch, and I fell in love with it. From then on, I got crab salad anytime and anywhere I could. When I went vegan, I tried the vegan crab and seafood salads from a bunch of different places, and nothing ever really tasted right. And then one day, it just kind of dawned on me that the texture of jackfruit might mix well with some hearts of palm and be a good substitute for seafood. So I tried it with all the regular ingredients that I would usually use in a seafood or crab salad, and honey, lo and behold, it was a winner.

Even though the only crab salad I eat now is this vegan one that I made up, I still always think of my childhood when I have it. Isn't it amazing how many memories are attached to food, and how it makes us feel when we indulge those memories? Seafood salad always gives me a good little flashback. I wonder what memories you'll make.

INGREDIENTS

Canned young green jackfruit

Jarred or canned sliced hearts of palm

Roughly chopped celery

Roughly chopped shallot

Snipped fresh chives

Vegan mayonnaise

Nori komi furikake seasoning

Garlic powder

Dried dill

Dried parsley

Fresh lemon juice

Sea salt

FOR SERVING

Old Bay seasoning* (optional)

Crackers

INSTRUCTIONS

DRAIN the jackfruit and hearts of palm in a colander. Rinse them well and drain again. You can squeeze the pieces of jackfruit to get some more of the brine out of it, if you want to. I always do.

TRANSFER the jackfruit and hearts of palm to a food processor. Add the celery, shallot, and chives and process on low or pulse just until coarsely chopped.

TRANSFER the mixture to a large bowl. Add mayonnaise, nori komi furikake, garlic powder, dill, parsley, lemon juice, and a pinch of salt and stir it all up together; you're looking for the texture of crab salad! Taste and add anything that's missing.

IT'S ready now, but if you want to, because it's your business, sprinkle a little Old Bay on top. Someone grab the crackers, and let's get into it!

Tabism: *Don't overthink today—just live in the moment!*

Remember—when using any seasoning that contains salt, don't be heavy-handed!

Lemon Pepper Potato Wedges with Blanch Dressing

Maybe you've heard me say it already, but my mama *loved* potatoes, and she passed that love on to me. Another thing I love very much is lemon pepper seasoning. Before I was vegan, I used to love lemon pepper wings served with ranch dressing. I mean, adding a little lemon pepper to anything makes it better, don't it? Any time I can add lemon pepper to something that also gives as much comfort as a potato does, it's a win for me. I would eat these potato wedges with my old favorite, ranch dressing, if I could, but she's not vegan. So I made her a cousin named *blanch*. And that's how my lemon pepper potato wedges with blanch dressing came to be. Eating them is like getting a hug with every bite!

INGREDIENTS

Potatoes (*I love russets, red potatoes, and sweet potatoes cooked this way; use what you love*), scrubbed

Seasoning salt (*I like Lawry's*)

Lemon pepper seasoning

Garlic powder

Chili powder

FOR THE BLANCH DRESSING

Vegan mayonnaise

Garlic powder

Onion powder

Dried dill

Snipped fresh chives

Fresh lemon juice

Kelly's Lemon Pepper Parm or other lemon pepper seasoning, for serving

INSTRUCTIONS

PREHEAT your air fryer to 370°F.

SLICE the potatoes lengthwise into 8 wedges each. Put the potato wedges in a pot and fill with water to cover by 1 inch. Bring the water to a boil over medium heat and add some seasoning salt. Simmer for about 10 minutes, until tender but not completely cooked through when poked with a skewer or sharp knife.

DRAIN the potatoes and sprinkle lemon pepper, garlic powder, and a pinch of chili powder all over them.

PLACE the potatoes in your air fryer and cook until browned and crispy in spots, about 10 minutes, shaking the basket halfway through to move the wedges on the bottom to the top and vice versa.

MEANWHILE, make the blanch dressing: In a medium bowl, combine the mayonnaise, garlic powder, onion powder, dill, chives, and lemon juice.

WHEN the wedges are ready, transfer them to a serving bowl or platter and sprinkle some lemon pepper parm on top. Serve them with the blanch!

Tabism: *Don't run from your problems, honey. Sit down with them and have a little chat.*

Mac & Cheese

INGREDIENTS

Butternut squash, peeled, seeded, and cut into cubes (*the more you use, the sweeter the taste*)

Russet potato, peeled and cut into cubes

Salt-free garlic and herb seasoning (*I like McCormick*)

Uncooked macaroni noodles

Sea salt

Vegan butter

Unsweetened plain cashew or almond milk yogurt

Nutritional yeast

Vegan cheddar cheese shreds

Vegan mozzarella cheese shreds

Garlic powder

Vegetable broth

FOR SERVING

Sweet paprika (optional)

Sliced avocado (optional)

Sriracha (optional)

Everything bagel seasoning* (*I like McCormick*) (optional)

Remember—when using any seasoning that contains salt, don't be heavy-handed!

I think mac and cheese is probably a staple in every household, but this is especially true in the South. I know I've always loved it, so when I became vegan, I had to make sure I could not only make mac and cheese, but make it good enough that I would love it just as much as I always have. People have said to me, "Girl, if I can't have mac and cheese, I can't go vegan." I thought that if I could figure out a way to make vegan mac and cheese taste just as good as the regular version, I could help a lot of people on their journey. And I really have. A lot of people love my mac and cheese.

If you're in the South, you're probably baking your mac and cheese, because everyone is expecting that crispy, cheesy crust on top. But if you got hungry kids waiting, or if you're the one who's extra hungry, honey, you can just make it on the stovetop. (Photo on pages 86–87.)

INSTRUCTIONS

PUT the butternut squash and potato in a pot and add water to cover. Bring to a boil over medium heat. Add some seasoning to the boiling water (as much as you want, because that's your business). Boil until the squash and potatoes are very tender. Drain (a little moisture is fine), and sit to the side.

IF you're going to bake the mac and cheese, preheat the oven to 350°F. Butter a casserole or baking dish (a 9 × 13–inch pan is good if you're making a full pound of pasta).

BRING a pot of water to a boil and add your macaroni noodles. Add a little sea salt and seasoning to the boiling water. If you're going to serve these straight from the pot, cook until they're done like you like to eat them. If you're going to bake the mac and cheese, undercook them slightly (they'll cook a little more in the oven). Drain the noodles and set aside.

IN a large sauté pan, melt some butter over medium heat with the squash and potatoes. Add the yogurt, nutritional yeast, cheddar and mozzarella shreds, and some garlic powder. Cook, stirring, until the cheese has melted and the sauce is real creamy.

STIR in a little broth to loosen the sauce.

ADD the drained noodles to the cheese mixture and mix it all up well.

YOU can serve the mac and cheese now, and people, especially kids, will love it! But if you're baking it, transfer the noodles and sauce to the prepared casserole and scatter some more cheese on top, if you'd like. Bake for 30 to 45 minutes, until the cheese has melted and the mac and cheese gets a little crispness on top. That's the Southern way.

TOP with paprika, if you'd like to. And if you're feeling fancy, serve it up on plates with sliced avocado, sriracha, and everything bagel seasoning. That's a little California spin I do sometimes. Enjoy!

Tabism: *Dreams are made inside of us; the goal is to get 'em out. I believe in you!*

Mac & Cheese,
84

Who Made the Potato Salad?

Who made the potato salad? Growing up in my family, that was always the question, whether we were with Moma's mom—that was Granny—or my daddy's mama—she was Grandma Etta. Everybody always wants to know who made the potato salad, because it's just that important. If you're going to eat it, it *has* to be right.

Potato salad is one of those things that can be served in any season, right? It's great in the summer, for a Fourth of July cookout. It's great during the holidays, for Thanksgiving or Christmas. It's great at a birthday party or baby shower. And I'll ask again, don't we love potatoes? It is really one of those things that can be made and enjoyed year-round—but it better be done right. You don't ever want to be the person where they be like, "Who made the potato salad? Oh, Lord, not . . . Oh, Lord, nah, I'm all right. I ain't gonna have that." So make sure you make *this* potato salad so ain't nobody looking at you crazy!

INGREDIENTS

White potatoes, like Yukon Gold or another thin-skinned variety (*I don't peel them, but you can if you want to*)

Sea salt

Garlic powder

Vegan mayonnaise

Yellow mustard

Chopped white onion

Chopped celery

Sweet pickle relish

Onion powder

Pinch of black salt (kala namak; see page xviii)

Pinch of sugar

Ground black pepper

Smoked paprika, for serving

INSTRUCTIONS

PUT the potatoes in a large pot and add water to cover. Bring to a boil over medium heat and add some salt and garlic powder. Gently boil the potatoes until they are soft when pierced with a skewer or sharp knife. You make sure you cook them enough. You don't want to be the person who undercooks the potatoes for the potato salad.

DRAIN the potatoes and transfer them to a large bowl. Use a spoon to break them up as much as you like.

ADD your vegan mayonnaise, mustard, onion, celery, relish, garlic powder, a little bit of onion powder, just a pinch of black salt, a little pinch of sugar, a pinch of sea salt, and some pepper. Mix it together until well combined. Taste and adjust any seasoning you think it needs.

SPRINKLE the top with some smoked paprika, because it's cute and my mama used to do it like that.

PUT it in the refrigerator and let it chill. You're ready to go!

Tabism: *Throw salt over your left shoulder once in a while, just like Grandma did.*

Sautéed Hearts of Palm with Coconut

Hearts of palm are the tender core of some palm trees. Palms with only a single stem die once they're cut and the heart is removed, but multi-stem palms regenerate every two to three years. And doesn't that make you think? We *all* have multi stems. We have legs. We have arms. And so even those times when it feels like our heart has been ripped out of our chest from pain or loss, we still have the ability to keep moving forward, right? And sometimes it might take us two or three years to feel well again, or two or three days, or two or three months, or two or three minutes if we just calm down and breathe. But any time we are suffering from heartache or heartbreak, let us think about how we can regenerate, just like multi-stem palms. When we are troubled within our hearts, maybe we can look at this recipe and feel better about our situation, knowing that we, too, can be restored.

INGREDIENTS

Jarred or canned whole hearts of palm, drained

Grapeseed oil

Nori komi furikake seasoning

Garlic powder

Shredded coconut

INSTRUCTIONS

CUT the hearts of palm in half lengthwise.

HEAT some grapeseed oil in a large sauté pan over medium heat. Add the hearts of palm cut-side down. Sprinkle generously with nori komi furikake, a little garlic powder, and some shredded coconut. (Yes, honey, you could do this first on a platter, but this is how I do it.)

COOK until nice and brown on the bottom, about 5 minutes. Flip them over and sprinkle the nori komi furikake, garlic powder, and coconut on top. Cook until browned on the bottom, about 5 minutes.

HONEY, you're ready to eat!

Tabism: *A good cry never hurt nobody; just don't stay in that space for too long.*

Yam Halves Topped with Maple-Cinnamon Pecan Glaze

Growing up in the South, we'd have candied yams with tons of butter and sugar, and then we'd put a little bit of cinnamon on top with pecans. As I went on my healthier journey, I still wanted a good old candied yam sometimes, but I realized I don't need all that sugar. And so these yam halves came about as a sort of spin-off, a healthier alternative to the candied yams I grew up with. Mine are super simple, too. I just bake the yam, cut it in half, and top it with the things that we usually top candied yams with. I still get the same flavor, but it's so much healthier. Plus, yams are already sweet! We got to let the yam be great on his own!

INGREDIENTS

Yams
Chopped pecans
Vegan butter
Pure maple syrup
Ground cinnamon
Shredded coconut

INSTRUCTIONS

PREHEAT the oven to 375°F.

POKE the yams a few times with a sharp knife or a fork to let the heat get all the way in there. Put them on a sheet pan and bake until they're soft when you poke them with a knife or fork, 1 hour or so.

WHEN the yams are almost done, put the pecans, butter, syrup, and cinnamon in a saucepan. Cook over medium heat, stirring frequently, for 3 to 5 minutes to bring it all together, but make sure it doesn't get too thick and sticky. You still want it to pour.

REMOVE the yams from the oven, slice them in half the long way (be careful—they're hot!), and put them on plates.

POUR some of the pecan topping over each yam half. Sprinkle the coconut on top, and feel free to sprinkle on some extra cinnamon if you want to, because that's your business.

Tabism: *It didn't happen to you—it happened through you.*

Thanksgiving Dressing

This recipe and the rest of the recipes in this chapter are all about tradition. Dressing, collard greens, green beans, okra—I mean, these things are staples, and in Black families in the South, most of it is just coming right out of the garden. We start here with dressing, which of course we can't grow in the garden, but it's a must for Thanksgiving, Christmas, and Easter. Dressing is just one of those things where if you're thinking about the holiday table, you know dressing is on there somewhere. It just is.

So how about a vegan dressing that no one will guess is vegan? Let's get into it. (Photo on page 94.)

INGREDIENTS

Vegan butter, for the baking dish and for drizzling on top of the dressing, if you want

Vegan apple-sage sausage, like Field Roast Smoked Apple & Sage, cut into chunks

Grapeseed oil

Finely chopped onion

Finely chopped celery

Finely chopped white mushrooms

Garlic powder

Dried sage

Dried thyme

Dried rosemary

Dried parsley

Vegan dry bread cubes for stuffing

Vegetable broth

INSTRUCTIONS

PREHEAT the oven to 350°F. Lightly butter the bottom and sides of a 9 × 13–inch or other 3-quart baking dish.

PROCESS the sausage in the food processor until chopped up fine. Set aside.

HEAT the oil in a large sauté pan over medium heat. Add the onion, celery, and mushrooms. Sprinkle in some garlic powder, sage, thyme, rosemary, and parsley. Sauté for about 10 minutes, until the vegetables are softened. Don't it smell good, honey?

PUT the bread cubes in a large bowl. Add the sautéed vegetables and the sausage and some broth and mix it together. Your mixture should be moist but not sopping wet. Add more broth if you need to.

TRANSFER the dressing to your prepared baking dish and smooth the surface. If you want to, melt some vegan butter in the microwave and drizzle it all over the surface of the dressing.

COVER the dressing with aluminum foil. Bake for 40 minutes.

REMOVE the foil and bake for another 15 minutes, until very lightly browned on top. Now you're ready to serve it!

Tabism: *Gather with your loved ones and encourage each other to share new things you don't already know about one another.*

Air-Fried Okra, Shiitake Mushrooms, and Chickpeas

Honey, when I was little I hated okra. I didn't like all that slime. Then I discovered *fried* okra, and I was like, *Oohhh*. But I don't like to eat too much fried stuff. *Air-*fried stuff, on the other hand, is good with my spirit. And air-frying that okra with shiitake mushrooms and chickpeas? Well, that's three times good with my spirit!

The main trick with air-frying is to season everything real good. Then you can go about your business for ten to fifteen minutes, and you'll have a whole air-fried meal or side dish. It's just so quick. It's so convenient. And it's fulfilling and delicious. Plus, the air fryer gives the veggies a little bit of char, so it just looks like you really put a lot of time and effort into it. You can look a little fancy when you put it on your table, especially if you have guests.

INGREDIENTS

Fresh or frozen okra

Fresh shiitake mushrooms

Canned or cooked chickpeas, well drained and rinsed

Extra-virgin olive oil

Salt-free multi-spice seasoning (*I like Cooking with Greens No Salt Onion Black Pepper Blend, but you use what you've got*)

Garlic powder

Nori komi furikake seasoning

Sea salt

CLOCKWISE FROM TOP LEFT:
Green Beans, 96; Thanksgiving Dressing, 93; Air-Fried Okra, Shiitake Mushrooms, and Chickpeas, 95; and Stewed Collard Greens, 97

INSTRUCTIONS

PREHEAT your air fryer to 400°F or your oven to 425°F. If you're using the oven, line a sheet pan with aluminum foil or parchment paper.

SLICE up your okra (I do mine about ½-inch thick, but you do it how you like it) and put it in a big bowl.

REMOVE and discard the stems from the shiitakes. Slice the caps and put them in the bowl with the okra. Add the chickpeas in there, too.

ADD a little bit of oil—enough to lightly coat everything. Add some seasoning blend, garlic powder, nori komi furikake, and a pinch of sea salt.

NOW mix it all up and make sure the oil and seasonings are all over the vegetables and chickpeas. I like to use my hands, but you can use a big spoon if you want, that's your business.

TRANSFER to the air fryer bowl or to the lined sheet pan, if using the oven.

AIR-FRY until browned and crispy in parts, 10 to 15 minutes, or roast, uncovered, for 20 minutes, stirring halfway through.

DO you hear that crunch? Oh yeah, let's get into it and enjoy.

Tabism: *Look in your mirror and repeat after me: I am afraid, but I'm going to do it anyway!!*

Green Beans

I remember sitting on the front porch with my granny trimming green beans. She called it "snapping peas." I don't think I was trying hard to pay a lot of attention to all the details when I was a girl, but now when I think about green beans, I can go right back to sitting on that porch with Granny. I can smell the air and actually feel the beans between my fingers as I snap them. I can see my great-granddaddy coming up in his old truck and talking to my granny outside in the front yard while we kept on snapping peas. Oh, I remember those days so clearly.

These are things that are just a part of who we are as Southerners, but they make the most amazing memories. I'm sure people all over the world eat these things. But there's something about being in the country, honey, on a good old Saturday morning, snapping peas with my granny and knowing that this is what we're going to eat for Sunday dinner, you know?

I love all beans, but growing up I really loved string beans (that's what we called them). Now that I'm an adult and a mom, what I love the most about green beans is that my son loves them. Mind you, they've got to be done just right, with all the juice cooked out of them, but when they're right, he loves them. And I'm just happy that he enjoys eating something green. (Photo on page 94.)

INGREDIENTS

Fresh or frozen green beans, trimmed and halved if fresh

Extra-virgin olive oil

Coconut aminos, liquid aminos, or soy sauce

Apple cider vinegar

Garlic powder

Nori komi furikake seasoning

Sliced tomatoes, for serving

INSTRUCTIONS

PUT the beans in a large sauté pan with a tight-fitting lid set over medium-low heat.

POUR a little oil, coconut aminos, and vinegar on top. Sprinkle on some garlic powder and nori komi furikake. Stir everything all together.

COVER and cook for 20 to 30 minutes, until the beans are tender and the liquid has reduced. Serve with sliced tomatoes, if you have them.

Tabism: *I know some days get tough, but don't give up!!*

Stewed Collard Greens

When I was growing up, we had greens all year long—mostly mustards and turnip greens. But on holidays, and especially New Year's Day, it was collards, served with black-eyed peas. We ate them for money and luck in the new year. And there was always something about how shiny the collard greens were that made me feel sure good luck was coming.

My husband loves greens, especially collards. It seems like it's just automatic in the Black community to make collards with pork or turkey to season the broth. I feel like it's part of our culture, almost a given, that we know how to make stewed or sautéed collard greens the traditional way. So I had to master that thing, honey. I loved greens simmered with pork when I was growing up, but I stopped eating beef and pork when I was fifteen. So when I learned how to make greens on my own, I used turkey necks, and then later, turkey wings, for a healthier option than pork.

And then I became vegan and figured out that I can make delicious collards with onions and garlic and vegetable broth and no meat at all. It's nice to be able to go right on loving this Southern favorite. Now when I eat collards, I know I'm eating an option that's healthier for me, and that certainly does feel lucky. (Photo on page 94.)

INGREDIENTS

Collard greens, ribs removed, leaves chopped

Grapeseed oil

Vegan no-chicken broth

Coconut aminos, liquid aminos, or soy sauce

Apple cider vinegar

A dash of liquid smoke

Garlic powder or minced garlic

Salt-free multi-spice seasoning

Sliced tomato, for serving

INSTRUCTIONS

PUT the collards in a large sauté pan and add a drizzle of oil, some broth, coconut aminos (for a bit of meaty taste), a splash of vinegar, and a dash of liquid smoke. Sprinkle some garlic powder and multi-spice seasoning on top.

COOK over medium heat for 10 minutes, stirring occasionally.

SERVE with tomatoes, if you'd like.

Tabism: *It's all about you today, so at this very moment, think of a healthy fruit or veggie, and the first thing that comes to mind, have that today! You can even have more than one, because that's your business!*

main dishes

IN THE PREVIOUS CHAPTER I TALKED ABOUT HOW appetizers and sides are kind of like a warm-up act, right? Well, this is the chapter that holds the event you showed up for in the first place! So while everything else can be going on around them, the dishes in this chapter are the stars of the show. They hold the center spotlight for a reason. And sometimes the main dish can represent you and how you feel in a moment. This is often true for me—whether it's a feeling or a memory, what I'm feeling inside ends up reflected in what I cook for myself and my family. If the same is true for you and the main dish represents how you're feeling, that's your cooking business. It's your show, your moment, your time to shine.

So, are you ready? Good. Let's go on and get into these main dishes, shall we?

Nachos

INGREDIENTS

FOR THE "MEATY" TOPPING

Vegan sausages (*I like Field Roast Smoked Apple & Sage, but you use what you like*)

Roughly chopped bell peppers (*you can use a mix of colors, if you'd like*)

Roughly chopped purple (red) or white onion

Grapeseed oil

Low-salt or salt-free taco seasoning

Garlic powder

Dried cilantro or chopped fresh cilantro

FOR THE NACHO CHEESE SAUCE

Unsweetened plain cashew milk yogurt

Vegan cheddar cheese shreds (*I like Daiya for this dish*)

Kelly's Taco Tuesday Parm

Garlic powder

Unsweetened cashew milk or other plant milk

Sea salt, if needed

The first time I ever made nachos was when I was working my first job at Taco Bell, where I used to make Nachos BellGrande. That was my specialty and a personal favorite. I felt like I was the master of making them. When I became an adult, I made nachos at home using ground turkey, and they became a family favorite. So when I went vegan, I had to figure out how to make my special nachos for my family, and to scratch this itch I would get for them.

They're so good! I make nachos in different ways, sometimes using jackfruit or mushrooms as my "meat." But when I really want the taste of traditional nachos, I go with a store-bought meat replacement. The secret to all nachos is that cheese, right? Here it's all about making sure you stir the cheese sauce while it cooks so the cheese melts right. And once you've got the meat and cheese taken care of, you can put just about anything on vegan nachos that you'd put on regular ones. In our family, we eat these for a main dish, but of course nachos can really be served at so many different moments. They're a good party food and a great snack for the kids and their friends on a Friday or Saturday night, and they're always good to put out in front of the game on Sunday. (Photo on page 101.)

INSTRUCTIONS

MAKE the topping: Cut the sausage into large pieces and place them in a food processor or Ninja. Add the bell peppers and chopped onion. Process until the mixture is chopped medium-fine and looks kind of like ground meat. Don't overfill the processor; do this in batches, if necessary.

HEAT a little oil in a large skillet over medium heat. Transfer the sausage mixture to the skillet. Add some taco seasoning, garlic powder, and cilantro and sauté until the sausage and onions are lightly browned, 8 to 10 minutes. Season to your taste. Cover the pan to keep warm and set aside.

FOR EVERYTHING ELSE!

Tortilla chips

Black beans, drained and rinsed, or warmed vegan refried beans

Chopped purple (red) onion or green onion

Sliced black olives

Sliced pickled jalapeños, drained

Salsa or Pico de Gallo (page 60)

Guacamole (page 59)

Dried cilantro or chopped fresh cilantro, for serving (optional)

MAKE the cheese sauce: Put the yogurt, cheddar, Taco Tuesday seasoning, garlic powder, and a little bit of milk in a saucepan. Cook over medium heat, stirring, until the cheese has melted and the sauce comes together, about 10 minutes; the sauce should be pretty thick so it doesn't run all over the place when you put it on the chips, but if it's too thick to easily spoon, stir in a splash of milk. Taste and add a pinch of salt, if necessary.

FOR each serving, arrange some tortilla chips on a plate. Spread some of the "meat" on top of the chips. Add some beans. Pour your nacho cheese on top. Now add your other toppings, in any order you'd like: onion, black olives, jalapeños, salsa or pico de gallo, and guacamole. Sprinkle on a little cilantro, if you want to, and serve.

Tabism: *You gotta let it go, honey! You know what "it" is . . . You will waste too much time and energy on it today.*

BBQ Vegan Meatballs

I grew up loving BBQ meatballs. We always had them for parties, and my mom made them every year for Christmas Eve. When I had a family of my own, BBQ meatballs were so popular with my husband and kids that I began to serve them as a main dish in our house. You can stick little cocktail toothpicks in them, honey, to serve them as finger foods at a bridal shower or baby shower or wedding reception. They are the perfect fancy pairing with Saved Eggs (page 72); you can serve them on a hoagie like the Cheese*fake* Hoagie (page 57); or serve them for Sunday dinner with potatoes and green beans. Either way, they make you feel kind of fancy!

Even though I altered the recipe a few years ago when I stopped eating all meat, no one ever believes me when I tell them these are vegan.

INGREDIENTS

Roughly chopped red bell pepper

Roughly chopped yellow onion

Roughly chopped garlic

Vegan ground meat substitute, such as Lightlife Plant-Based Ground or Beyond (*I use about 1½ pounds for 12 to 16 meatballs*)

Garlic powder

Salt-free multi-spice seasoning

Grapeseed oil

Pure maple syrup

Your favorite vegan BBQ sauce (*I like Stubb's Smokey Brown Sugar; you use whatever you want, because that's your business*)

INSTRUCTIONS

PUT the bell pepper, onion, and garlic in a food processor or Ninja. Process until chopped small but not so much that the mixture becomes mush; leave a little texture in there. Do this in batches, if necessary.

TRANSFER the chopped vegetables to a large bowl and add the ground meat substitute. Sprinkle in some garlic powder and multi-spice seasoning. Use your hands to gently mix everything together.

ROLL the mixture into golf ball–size balls.

IN a large sauté pan with a lid, heat some oil over medium heat. Add your meatballs and cook, turning them occasionally, for 3 to 5 minutes, until they are evenly browned.

POUR a little maple syrup on the meatballs, then add enough BBQ sauce to coat all the meatballs and cover the bottom of the pan.

COVER the pan and cook, turning them occasionally, until cooked all the way through, 5 to 10 minutes.

SERVE and enjoy!

Tabism: *The only time people are negative is when someone or something has caused them pain or fear.*

Jackfruit Pot Roast

When I was a little girl, whether I was home or staying over at my granny's house, I would often wake up to the smell of pot roast simmering in the slow cooker with carrots and potatoes and onions. They would start it the night before or first thing in the morning, and the incredible smell would float through the whole house. That aroma was so comforting and made me feel so cozy. One day, long after I grew up and became a vegan, I remember thinking that I wanted that feeling again, you know? So I decided to make a pot roast myself, using jackfruit. And honey, that familiar, amazing smell literally woke me up in the middle of the night! Here are the vegetables I put in mine; you can put these in or choose others that are more familiar to you. Let your preferences determine the quantity of each veggie.

INGREDIENTS

Red potatoes, cut in half, or quartered if very big

Sliced or shredded fresh or frozen carrots

Sliced celery

Sweet onion, cut into wedges

Chopped garlic

Canned young green jackfruit, drained

Vegan no-chicken broth

Coconut aminos, liquid aminos, or soy sauce

Vegan bouillon base, such as Better Than Bouillon seasoned vegetable base

A dash of liquid smoke

Dried thyme, rosemary, and/or sage

Garlic powder

Salt-free multi-spice seasoning

Sea salt

Ground black pepper

INSTRUCTIONS

PUT the potatoes, carrots, celery, onion, and garlic in a slow cooker. Add the jackfruit.

POUR in enough broth to barely cover the vegetables. Add some coconut aminos, bouillon base, and a dash of liquid smoke. Sprinkle in some dried herbs, garlic powder, seasoning spice, and a pinch each of salt and black pepper.

STIR to combine. Cover and cook on low for 5 to 7 hours. The stew will be ready to eat after 5 hours, but the great thing about cooking jackfruit in the slow cooker is that it won't do any harm to leave it longer, if that's more convenient for you—and it keeps that good aroma in the kitchen.

TASTE and adjust the seasoning. Serve very warm.

Tabism: *Today, treat yourself to a lollipop, but don't bite it—be patient and enjoy it awhile.*

Vallops (Vegan Scallops)

Before I was vegan, whenever anybody ever asked me what my favorite food was, the answer was seafood. Now when people ask me what my favorite food is, I say I don't have one.

And that's okay. Sometimes we have a favorite thing that we think we cannot live without. But then a change will happen, and we *must* learn to live without it. And then we realize that— guess what?—we *can* live without it. We find out there is a better option. Or sometimes we figure out that there isn't a *better* option, but there *is* a suitable one. I loved seafood, and I guess I still do, even though I don't eat it anymore.

I'm just so grateful that I figured out a way to make "vallops," or vegan scallops, using trumpet mushrooms. They scratch the itch and fill the craving whenever I have it. Honey, that's why we praise the Lord for trumpet mushrooms, and we thank God for these vallops. Serve them with whatever you'd serve scallops with, like a salad or a baked potato and sautéed spinach.

INGREDIENTS

King trumpet mushrooms

Extra-virgin olive oil

Salt-free garlic and herb seasoning (*I like McCormick*)

Greek seasoning

Old Bay seasoning*

Nori komi furikake seasoning

1 stick (8 tablespoons) vegan butter

Chopped garlic

Remember—when using any seasoning that contains salt, don't be heavy-handed!

INSTRUCTIONS

WIPE the mushrooms clean with a damp cloth. Slice them crosswise (not too thin or thick—remember, we want them to resemble scallops). Keep the caps and cook them right alongside the vallops. Don't make the cap feel bad because it looks different; it tastes just as good as the rest of the mushroom!

PUT the mushroom slices and caps in a large bowl. Pour a little olive oil on top and sprinkle on as much garlic and herb seasoning, Greek seasoning, Old Bay seasoning, and nori komi furikake as you want. Stir the mushrooms around gently (I use my hands) to coat with the seasoning.

HEAT a well-seasoned cast-iron grill pan or skillet over medium-high heat. Add the seasoned mushrooms to the pan in a single layer and sear on each side until brown.

MEANWHILE, melt your butter in a small saucepan over medium-low heat. Add the garlic and a bit of Old Bay seasoning and stir to combine. Simmer for 30 to 60 seconds to lightly cook the garlic.

BRUSH the garlic butter on both sides of the vallops and mushroom caps.

TRANSFER the vallops to plates or a serving platter and drizzle the rest of the garlic butter on top, if you please.

Tabism: *You already have what you need inside.*

Tab's Traditional Lasagna

Pasta can satisfy all sorts of different taste buds. Some people love skinny noodles. Some people love thick noodles. Some people love elbow noodles. And then there are others who don't or can't actually eat any shape of pasta, but they love pasta-style dishes, so things like zucchini noodles are a gift to them. The great thing in our house is there's at least a few versions of lasagna and other pasta dishes that we all love. I share some of them on the next several pages, beginning with this family favorite, my traditional vegan lasagna. My husband loves it. Choyce loves it. All my friends love it. I make it for big gatherings because it goes a long way. It's a comfort food, it's packed with veggies, and when I use vegan Italian sausage, honey, no one misses a thing.

INGREDIENTS
FOR THE FILLING

Vegan Italian sausage, chopped

Roughly chopped green bell pepper

Roughly chopped red bell pepper

Roughly chopped purple (red) onion

Sliced mushrooms

Baby spinach

Extra-virgin olive oil

Garlic powder

Salt-free multi-spice seasoning

FOR THE LASAGNA

No-bake lasagna noodles, such as gluten-free green lentil or regular lasagna noodles

1 large jar marinara sauce

Vegan pepper Jack cheese shreds

Vegan mozzarella cheese shreds

Vegan cheddar cheese shreds

Dried basil, oregano, or whatever herbs you like

INSTRUCTIONS

PREHEAT the oven to 400°F. Lightly oil a 9 × 13–inch baking pan.

MAKE the filling: Put the sausage, bell peppers, onion, mushrooms, and spinach in a food processor or Ninja. Process until it's all chopped up like ground meat. Don't overfill the machine; do this in batches, if necessary.

HEAT a little bit of oil in a large skillet over medium heat. Transfer the filling to the pan and add some garlic powder and multi-spice seasoning. Cook, stirring occasionally, until lightly browned, 12 to 15 minutes. Season to taste.

ASSEMBLE the lasagna: Arrange your first layer of slightly overlapping noodles in the bottom of the prepared pan, using up to half the noodles in the box.

SPREAD half the filling over the noodles. Cover the filling with a layer of marinara sauce, using up to half of what you have.

SPRINKLE the cheese over the sauce, using up to half of what you have. Arrange a second layer of noodles over the cheese. Spread the remaining filling on top.

COVER the filling with marinara, then sprinkle cheese on top. If you'd like, you can sprinkle on some of your multi-spice seasoning or dried herbs or both.

COVER the pan with aluminum foil and bake for 30 to 40 minutes (depending on what type of noodles you have; take a look at what the box says for cooking time).

UNCOVER the pan and bake for 5 to 10 minutes more to get the cheese on top nice and melted. Let stand for a few minutes before serving!

Tabism: *Remember, "No" is a complete sentence.*

Eggplant Lasagna

INGREDIENTS

Raw cashews, about
2 cups for a lasagna
this size

FOR THE LASAGNA

Eggplant, about 3
pounds total for a 9- or
10-inch-deep baking
pan, or about 4 pounds
total for a deep 9 × 13–
inch pan (*if you want
leftovers*)

Zucchini

Summer squash

Red bell pepper

Green bell pepper

Sweet onions

White mushrooms

Extra-virgin olive oil

Salt-free garlic and
herb seasoning (*I like
McCormick*)

Italian seasoning

Onion powder

Sea salt

Baby spinach

Fresh lemon juice

Canned chopped stewed
tomatoes, drained

FOR THE CHEESE SAUCE

Minced garlic

Nutritional yeast

Unsweetened plain
cashew milk yogurt

Salt-free garlic and
herb seasoning (*I like
McCormick*)

Onion powder

I created this recipe as a healthier option for the people in my life who don't eat gluten. Instead of using processed, gluten-free lasagna noodles, I use sliced eggplant. Now, the key to success here is to make sure you thoroughly drain the eggplant on paper towels and cook out the liquid from it as well as from the zucchini and summer squash. These veggies hold so much water, and it will make your lasagna soggy if you aren't careful.

INSTRUCTIONS

PREHEAT the oven to 375°F. Lightly oil a deep 9- or 10-inch square or 9 × 13–inch rectangular baking dish.

PUT the cashews in a bowl and pour warm water over them to cover by about 2 inches. Set aside for 30 minutes to soften.

MEANWHILE, prepare the lasagna vegetables: Cut the eggplant lengthwise into slices about ¼-inch thick. Lay the slices out on paper towels to absorb their moisture. Set aside while you prepare the other ingredients.

CUT the zucchini and summer squash into chunks. Remove the seeds and ribs from the bell peppers and cut the peppers into thick slices. Slice the onions and mushrooms.

PUT the zucchini, summer squash, bell peppers, onions, and half the mushrooms in a food processor or Ninja (set the rest of the mushrooms aside). Process until finely chopped. Don't overfill the processor; do this in batches, if necessary.

HEAT a little oil in a large skillet over medium heat. Add the chopped vegetables and sprinkle in the garlic and herb and Italian seasonings, onion powder, and a pinch of sea salt.

SAUTÉ until the mixture is fragrant, the liquid has evaporated, and the vegetables are taking on some color, 12 to 15 minutes. Season to taste. Scrape the vegetables into a bowl and set aside.

WIPE out the skillet. Add a little oil to the skillet and heat over medium heat. Add the reserved mushrooms and sprinkle them with some garlic and herb and Italian seasonings. Sauté until lightly browned, 4 to 6 minutes.

ADD a few or several handfuls of spinach and sprinkle in a little more of your seasonings. Cook, stirring frequently, until wilted, about 1 minute. Season to taste. Remove from the heat and set aside.

HEAT a well-seasoned cast-iron grill pan over medium heat.

PAT the eggplant slices dry. Drizzle on some oil and lemon juice and sprinkle with some garlic and herb seasoning.

COOK the eggplant slices a few at a time on the hot grill pan until there are brown grill marks on both sides, about 2 minutes per side. Set aside.

MAKE the cheese sauce: Drain the cashews and transfer them to a food processor. Add the garlic (a little or a lot, that's your business), nutritional yeast, yogurt, and garlic and herb seasoning and onion powder. Process until well blended. Season to taste. Set aside.

ARRANGE 3 or 4 eggplant slices (no more than one-third the total number of slices) over the bottom of the prepared pan.

SPREAD half the chopped vegetable mixture on top of the eggplant.

SPREAD half the sautéed mushroom and spinach on top of the chopped vegetables.

SCATTER half the tomatoes on top of the mushrooms and spinach.

SPOON one-third to half the cheese sauce on top of the tomatoes (use one-third of the cheese sauce if you want to have some left over for the top of the lasagna; use half if you want your top layer to be eggplant only—either way is fine, honey). Don't worry about spreading it evenly.

ARRANGE half the remaining eggplant slices on top of the cheese sauce. Layer on the remaining chopped vegetables, sautéed mushrooms and spinach, and tomatoes.

ON top of the vegetables, spoon half or all the remaining cheese sauce, depending on whether you want to have some left to top the lasagna or not.

ARRANGE the final layer of eggplant on top of the cheese sauce. If you have more cheese sauce left, you can spread it on top of the lasagna.

BAKE for about 30 minutes or until it starts to brown and is tender when pierced in the center with a thin, sharp knife. Let stand for 15 to 20 minutes before serving, with a salad if you want one.

Tabism: *"I changed my mind" is a complete sentence.*

Creamy Garlic Basil Zucchini "Pasta"

So here's a low-carb, gluten-free option for people who are trying to stay away from starches and heavy carbs but still want to eat something delicious. The basil and garlic are just such a good combination and satisfying to all sorts of taste buds. Take my son, Quest, who once declared that he rated it a nine out of ten. Honey! When a child gives something a nine out of ten, you *know* it's very good!

I use a Veggetti Pro to spiralize the zucchini for this dish, but there are lots of other spiralizers on the market (or you can buy ready-to-go spiralized zucchini in the produce section of the grocery store). (Photo on pages 116–17.)

INGREDIENTS

Grapeseed oil

Chopped cremini mushrooms

Chopped garlic

Greek seasoning

Unsweetened plain cashew milk yogurt

Vegan parmesan cheese shreds

Chopped fresh basil, plus some for serving

2 large or 4 medium zucchini, spiralized

Fresh lemon juice

Crushed red pepper flakes, for serving (optional)

INSTRUCTIONS

IN a large skillet with a tight-fitting lid, heat a little oil over medium heat. Add the mushrooms, garlic, and a little bit of Greek seasoning. Cook, stirring, until the mushrooms are lightly browned.

ADD a couple spoonfuls of yogurt, a handful of parmesan, and a handful of chopped basil. Stir to combine and cook, stirring, until the cheese has melted and there's a little bit of creamy sauce in the pan. Turn the heat down if it's cooking too quickly. The sauce should not be too liquidy; if it is, stir in a little more cheese and simmer it very gently to thicken it up. Taste and adjust the seasoning.

ADD the zucchini and stir or use tongs to gently coat the zucchini noodles and mushrooms with the sauce. Add a little more seasoning.

COVER the pan and cook for 5 minutes.

UNCOVER and squeeze in some lemon juice to taste. Adjust the seasoning, if necessary.

TOP each serving with a little chopped basil and some red pepper flakes, if you want a little kick of heat. Enjoy!

Tabism: *Hug yourself today and know that all is well.*

Chance's Sausage
and Veggie Pasta,
118

Creamy Garlic
Basil Zucchini
"Pasta," 115

Bow Ties
Alfredo, 119

Chance's Sausage and Veggie Pasta

Chance loves this so much that he learned how to make it himself! Can you think of better proof that it's quick, easy, filling, and delicious? (Photo on page 116.)

INGREDIENTS

Spaghetti noodles

Vegan Italian sausage, such as Field Roast, sliced

Vegetable broth

Salt-free garlic and herb seasoning (*I like McCormick*)

Zucchini, sliced into half-moons

Sliced white mushrooms

Chopped garlic

Bagged kale and chard blend, finely chopped

About half a 15-ounce can diced tomatoes with their juice (*or use the whole can if you want to*)

Sea salt

Ground black pepper

Fresh lemon juice

Kelly's Roasted Garlic Parm or other seasoning, for serving

INSTRUCTIONS

BRING a large pot of water to a boil. Cook the spaghetti according to the package instructions. Drain and set aside.

MEANWHILE, put the sausage in a large skillet. Pour in enough broth to just cover the bottom of the pan. Add some garlic and herb seasoning. Cook over medium heat until the sausage is lightly browned in spots, flipping it occasionally, about 5 minutes.

ADD the zucchini, mushrooms, and garlic to the skillet and cook, stirring occasionally, until the vegetables are tender and the sausage is lightly browned on both sides, 5 to 10 minutes. Add a little more broth if the sausage or vegetables begin to stick to the bottom of the pan.

IF the pan is completely dry, add a little more broth, then add the kale and chard to the pan. Add some more seasoning and cook, stirring, until the greens are cooked down a little, about 2 minutes.

ADD the tomatoes with their juice and cook down for about 5 minutes, so the tomatoes can join the party. Add a little salt and pepper and a splash of lemon juice. Taste and add more of any seasoning you think it needs.

TO serve, swirl some pasta on each plate. Spoon some sausage and veggie mix on top. Sprinkle on some roasted garlic parm, if you'd like, and eat very, very good.

Tabism: *How do you know if you've never tried?*

Bow Ties Alfredo

A classic Alfredo sauce is creamy and delicious. And so is a vegan Alfredo sauce! This dish is fun to make with kids, who love the little bow ties. Choyce really loves it. (Photo on page 117.)

INGREDIENTS

FOR THE PASTA AND VEGGIES

Bow ties (farfalle), or whatever pasta you like

Vegetable broth or olive oil

Summer squash, sliced into half-moons

Zucchini, sliced into half-moons

Sliced red bell pepper

Smallish broccoli florets

Dried basil

Garlic powder

Lemon pepper seasoning

Pinch of sea salt

FOR THE ALFREDO SAUCE

1 stick (8 tablespoons) vegan butter

Chopped garlic

Unsweetened plain cashew milk yogurt

Vegan parmesan cheese shreds

Dried basil

Garlic powder

INSTRUCTIONS

BRING a large pot of water to a boil and cook your pasta according to the package directions. Drain and set aside.

MEANWHILE, pour some broth or olive oil into a large skillet over medium heat. Add the summer squash, zucchini, bell pepper, and broccoli. Sprinkle on as much dried basil, garlic powder, and lemon pepper as you want and add a pinch of sea salt. Stir it all up and cook until the veggies are tender, 5 to 7 minutes.

TRANSFER the veggies to a bowl and set aside.

MAKE your Alfredo sauce: Wipe out the skillet and melt a stick of butter over medium heat. Add the garlic and let it cook for a few seconds so you can smell it.

ADD some big spoonfuls of yogurt and a handful of parmesan, then add some dried basil and garlic powder. Stir it all up until the cheese has melted and you have a creamy sauce. Taste and adjust the seasoning.

ADD your pasta and cooked veggies and stir it up. Honey, you're done!

Tabism: *Today I encourage you to dress the way you want to feel!*

Maple BBQ Kebabs

INGREDIENTS

Fresh pineapple, cut into 1-inch chunks

Zucchini, halved lengthwise and sliced into ½-inch-thick half-moons

White mushrooms, cut in half

Red bell pepper, cut into 1-inch pieces

Green bell pepper, cut into 1-inch pieces

Canned young green jackfruit, very well drained

Purple (red) onion, cut into wedges

Garlic powder

Salt-free multi-spice seasoning

Sea salt

Ground black pepper

Fresh lemon juice

Pure maple syrup

Grapeseed oil, for the grill

Your favorite vegan BBQ sauce

Equipment: Bamboo or metal skewers*

If you're using bamboo skewers, soak them in a pan of water while you're preparing the fruit and vegetables; this helps prevent them from burning on the grill.

Kebabs are great any time of the year, but they are especially fun in the summertime. You can put all sorts of veggies and fruit on a skewer and have a little fun on the grill. And you know Jack (that's jackfruit) is one of my favorite ingredients to include in kebabs. He be out here winning Oscars, acting like he's chicken or pork, even though he's not. One thing for sure is that Jack is always delicious if seasoned and cooked right.

INSTRUCTIONS

PUT the pineapple, zucchini, mushrooms, bell peppers, jackfruit, and onion in a large bowl. Season with a little or a lot of the garlic powder and multi-spice seasoning. Add a little salt and black pepper. Squeeze in some lemon juice and pour some maple syrup over the mixture. Use your hands or a big spoon to gently stir the ingredients around until they are well coated with seasonings.

TASTE a piece to see if you think it has enough seasoning. Go ahead and add anything you think it needs, honey.

THREAD the vegetables and jackfruit onto skewers in any alternating order you like. I like to start each kebab with a piece of bell pepper because it's sturdy and acts like a gate, stopping all the other fruits and vegetables from sliding off the skewers.

PREPARE a hot grill; if the spaces between the slats on your grill grate are wide, you can cover the grate with heavy-duty aluminum foil or copper grill mats (they're sold in hardware stores and online) before you light it. Lightly brush the grill grate, foil, or grill mat with oil.

BRUSH the kebabs with BBQ sauce and put them sauce-side down on the grill. Cook until they are nicely browned in spots, 8 to 10 minutes. Brush them with BBQ sauce, then flip them and grill on the other side until nicely browned, another 8 to 10 minutes.

REMOVE the kebabs from the grill and place on a platter. Serve and enjoy!

Tabism: *Think of an old nursery rhyme that reminds you of your childhood! Say it out loud and give yourself a trip down memory lane.*

Country-Style Steak with Gravy

I went to Burton Grove Elementary School in Eden, North Carolina, when I was growing up, and then Intermediate School for fifth and sixth grades. I loved school lunch, and oh my goodness, country-style steak with gravy served with potatoes and some green beans was one of my favorites. I was one of those (probably a little weird) kids who would say, "Oohhh, it's country-style-steak day!" I just loved it.

Food is always associated with memories for me, and when I miss the feeling of my inner child sometimes, country-style steak with gravy gives that back to me. Also, my husband loves it, and you know I'm a real Southern woman at heart who loves to cook for my family, and especially my husband. I get excited to see him eat and enjoy his food, and he *loves* a good plate smothered in gravy. It is some "good eatin'." It makes me feel like I'm in third grade again and I've got no worries. Life is grand!

INGREDIENTS

Grapeseed oil

Vegetable broth

Sliced white mushrooms

Sliced white onion

Garlic powder

Salt-free multi-spice seasoning

Vegan burgers, such as Field Roast Chef's Signature burgers (*about 1 per person*)

All-purpose flour or other flour

INSTRUCTIONS

POUR a little oil and some broth into a large skillet. Add the mushrooms and onion and set over medium heat. Sprinkle on some garlic powder and multi-spice seasoning and cook, stirring, until softened, 2 to 5 minutes.

PUSH the vegetables to the side and add your burgers to the pan. The broth should come up to the top of them but not cover them; add more broth, if necessary. Cook until the burgers are heated through, about 5 minutes.

MEANWHILE, combine about 3 tablespoons each of flour and broth in a small bowl. Use a fork to mix until smooth.

POUR this mixture into the pan and stir it into the broth. Cook until it thickens; if it's too thick, add some more broth; if it's too thin, stir up some more flour and broth and stir it in. Once the sauce is at the right thickness for your taste, let it bubble for about 1 minute to cook out any floury taste. Taste the sauce and adjust the seasoning. Serve hot!

Tabism: *I know you've been hurt before, but you can't guard your heart forever. You deserve to be loved, and I know you have so much love to give.*

Vegan Sausage and Cabbage

Sausage and cabbage is such an old-school Southern meal. My granny made it all the time when I was growing up, but I kind of forgot about it when I became an adult. Then, when I was pregnant with my son, my mother-in-law (hey, Zane!) came from North Carolina to stay with us, and she started making it for us using turkey sausage. And I was like, "Oh my God, I used to love this so much! How did I forget about it?" Then I began to actually crave it, especially how she served it, with sliced tomato and cornbread on the side. Honestly, it was one of the only things I craved when I was pregnant with Quest that wasn't junk food. Plus, I loved the way it would take me back to those great feelings from my childhood.

More recently, I found myself craving it one day, so I made it this vegan way and it became a favorite all over again. My husband enjoys it and Choyce loves it, but honestly, this one is really more about me. It's just one of those quick, easy meals that tastes so good!

The one important thing you've got to remember is that you've got to be a little heavy-handed with the black pepper, which just does something special for this dish. Plus, that's how my granny did it.

INGREDIENTS

Sausage links, such as Field Roast or Beyond Sausage, or your favorite vegan sausage (*I figure 1 sausage per person*)

Grapeseed oil or vegetable broth (*your choice*)

Chopped white onion

Garlic powder

Salt-free multi-spice seasoning (*I like Cooking with Greens No Salt Onion Black Pepper Blend, but you use what you've got*)

Ground black pepper

Cabbage (*green or red, that's your business*)

Chopped red bell pepper

INSTRUCTIONS

SLICE the sausage and put it in a large sauté pan with a tight-fitting lid. Add a little oil or broth.

ADD your chopped onion and some garlic powder if you'd like, because that's your business. Add your seasoning blend and black pepper to the pan as well.

WHILE this is starting to cook, rinse your cabbage and chop it however you please (big pieces, little pieces, it doesn't matter—you eat it the way you like it).

TAKE a look at your sausage. When it's browning and pretty cooked throughout, add a few handfuls of the cabbage to the pan and season it with some more garlic powder, seasoning blend, and black pepper. Use tongs or a big spoon to mix it around so it wilts a little and makes room for some more.

AFTER you mix all that cabbage in there, add the bell pepper. Cover and cook for 5 to 10 minutes, until the peppers are softened. If the food starts to stick to the pan, add a little more oil or broth to help unstick it. Season to taste.

FOR SERVING

Cucumber

A little apple cider vinegar

Pinch of sea salt

Ground black pepper

Sliced tomato

WHILE the cabbage and sausage are finishing up, slice up some cucumber and put it in a bowl. Top it with a little apple cider vinegar, a pinch of salt, and some black pepper. Stir it up, then taste and adjust the seasoning.

TO serve, spoon some sausage and cabbage onto plates. Add some seasoned cucumber and sliced tomato on the side and sprinkle some salt and black pepper on the tomato. Enjoy!

Tabism: *Just because things don't look like they will work out doesn't mean they won't. Keep going!*

Moma's Meatloaf

Two 1-pound packs vegan ground meat substitute, such as Beyond, Impossible, or Lightlife (*you can use just one pack if you don't want leftovers*)

Chopped sweet onion

Chopped red bell pepper

Chopped green bell pepper

Salt-free multi-spice seasoning

Garlic powder

Bread crumbs

About 2 teaspoons ground flaxseed

Coconut aminos, liquid aminos, or soy sauce

Yellow mustard

Brown sugar

FOR THE TOPPING

(*I do it all from the spirit, but let's say about . . .*)

1 cup ketchup

2 tablespoons yellow mustard

2 tablespoons brown sugar

2 teaspoons pure maple syrup (optional)

Nobody made meatloaf like my mama. Her ketchup topping was always the perfect color. Every bite had a wonderful sweetness, but it was also savory. I think her secret was a little bit of mustard.

I feel like I can taste it right this minute. For years I made a version of her meatloaf using ground turkey. And then when I went vegan it was one of the very first things I looked into making in a new way. I'll be honest, Chance is not a big meatloaf person at all, and the kids think it's fine but not amazing. This vegan meatloaf is really all about me, because it makes me think of Moma. And when I eat it, it's like I can feel my legs swinging in my chair at the table. I always have danced when I eat—that's how you know it's good! I remember being maybe five years old and my feet couldn't even touch the ground. And when Moma made meatloaf, I'd be dancing in my chair with my feet swinging. I was so excited sitting at the dinner table eating my meatloaf. Yes, this one brings a memory in every bite.

INSTRUCTIONS

PREHEAT the oven to 375°F.

PUT your ground meat substitute in a large bowl. Add some onion and bell peppers.

SPRINKLE on some multi-spice seasoning and garlic powder and add a handful of bread crumbs, the ground flaxseed, and 2 to 3 tablespoons water.

DRIZZLE in some coconut aminos, squeeze the mustard on, and add a handful of brown sugar.

USE a spoon or your hands to mix all the ingredients together. Evenly pat the mixture into a deep 9- or 10-inch square baking pan.

MAKE the topping: In a small bowl, mix the topping ingredients until well combined. Pour the topping over the loaf and smooth out the top.

BAKE for 1 hour, until the meatloaf is firm and the edges are slightly browned. Let cool in the pan for about 10 minutes, then cut into squares and serve.

Tabism: *Put yourself first. It's not selfish. It's self-care.*

Fried "Fish" with Tartar Sauce

Hearts of palm make the most amazing substitute for fish in vegan fish sticks. They are spot-on with the flakiness, the texture, and the crispiness when fried right. My husband loves these. My kids love these. My friends love these. They cook up really well in the air fryer. They do well deep-fried. They do well pan-fried on the stovetop. And they do well whether you batter them before dipping in the seasoned breadcrumbs or not.

Like I said, honey, these are the most amazing vegan fish sticks.

INGREDIENTS

1 jar or can (or more) whole hearts of palm

Ready-to-use vegan fish fry (seafood breading mix), such as Bamma Fish Fry

Nori komi furikake seasoning

Garlic powder

Old Bay seasoning*

Dried dill

Grapeseed oil, for frying

FOR THE TARTAR SAUCE

Vegan mayonnaise

Dried dill

Garlic powder

Sweet pickle relish

Chili-garlic sauce (*I like Huy Fong*; optional)

Remember—when using any seasoning that contains salt, don't be heavy-handed!

INSTRUCTIONS

DRAIN the hearts of palm and lay them out on a work surface. Working with one at a time, poke a fork in at one end and pull and poke it down the length of the heart of palm, opening it up and shredding the top a bit. Don't shred it too much or poke too deep into the heart of palm; you want it to hold together. Repeat with the remaining hearts of palm.

POUR some fish fry into a medium bowl.

PLACE the hearts of palm in another medium bowl. Season generously with nori komi furikake and garlic powder, then sprinkle on some Old Bay and dill. Gently turn and flip the hearts of palm to cover them evenly with the seasoning, then transfer them to the fish fry and turn to coat evenly.

POUR enough oil into a deep frying pan that it will mostly cover the hearts of palm once you've added them. Be sure the pan is tall enough that the oil can't escape! Heat the oil over medium-high heat until very hot and shimmery.

CAREFULLY add the hearts of palm, a few at a time, and fry until deep golden brown on both sides, 1 to 2 minutes per side. Transfer them to paper towels to drain.

OH, wait a minute! I can't forget the tartar sauce: Mix together some vegan mayo, dill, and some garlic powder. Add some sweet relish and, if you like some kick, a little chili-garlic sauce. Mix it together, taste, and season it to how you like it. Now you have your tartar. Serve it with your fried fish sticks!

Tabism: *Baby, put your favorite song on and turn it up! Sing, dance, cry, laugh, and most of all, remember you are alive!*

Crab-less Cakes with Spicy Tartar Sauce

INGREDIENTS

Oyster or enoki mushrooms

Canned or jarred artichoke hearts, marinated or in brine, drained

Cooked or canned chickpeas (*just a bit, honey*), drained and rinsed

Roughly chopped green bell pepper

Roughly chopped red bell pepper

Roughly chopped celery

Roughly chopped green onion

Panko bread crumbs

Salt-free garlic and herb seasoning (*I like McCormick*)

Old Bay seasoning*

Nori komi furikake seasoning

Dried dill

Sea salt

Ground black pepper

Fresh lemon juice

Grapeseed oil

Spicy tartar sauce (see page 127; *use the chili-garlic sauce for this one, honey, it's supposed to be spicy!*), for serving

Remember—when using any seasoning that contains salt, don't be heavy-handed!

These are one of my most favorite things. I have so many different recipes for vegan crab cakes because I miss them so much and have tried everything to get that taste exactly right. You know I miss all seafood, but oohhh, honey, crab was really Tab's thing. So when I figured out how to replace crab with other ingredients, like mushrooms, artichoke hearts, hearts of palm, and jackfruit, it did my heart so proud. And honey, if you add a little Old Bay, it'll make you feel like you back in the sea. Like I want to sing, *"Under the sea, honey, under the sea."* You might start singing, too, while you eat these! And if you do, that's your business. Okay? Okay.

INSTRUCTIONS

PREHEAT your air fryer to 400°F or your oven to 425°F.

WIPE the mushrooms clean with a damp cloth. Put them in a food processor or Ninja along with the artichoke hearts, chickpeas, bell peppers, celery, and green onion. Process until chopped. Don't overblend; you want the mixture to be flaky, not mushy. Do this in batches, if necessary.

TRANSFER the mixture to a large bowl. Add a couple handfuls of panko, some garlic and herb seasoning, a sprinkle of Old Bay, nori komi furikake, dried dill, a pinch of salt, and some black pepper. Add a splash of lemon juice and some oil. Mix everything together and use your hands to form the mixture into patties that are 2 to 3 inches across. If the mixture seems too dry, mix in some more oil or lemon juice. If it seems too moist, mix in some more panko.

PLACE the patties in the air fryer or on a baking sheet if using the oven. Air-fry for 10 to 15 minutes, until browned, checking the patties every 5 minutes. If using the oven, bake the patties until firm, 10 to 15 minutes, then flip and bake until browned, about 15 minutes.

SERVE the crab-less cakes hot, with spicy tartar sauce alongside.

Tabism: *Sing out loud in your shower today, and if you've already taken one, take the stage in your car, honey!!*

Cast-Iron Oyster Mushrooms and Mango

Do you ever feel like you want to get away, even if you can't literally leave your kitchen? This is the dish to make when that feeling hits, because the smell and sound of mangoes and mushrooms sizzling on a grill pan will take you to a summertime paradise, even if it's the middle of winter. It'll be like you're on a little tropical island, and honey, you might put on a doggone straw hat and get to cooking in your kitchen with a bathing suit on, if that's your business. At the very least, I hope you feel just as happy as I do when I make and eat this delicious meal.

INGREDIENTS

Oyster mushrooms

Whole mango

Salt-free garlic and herb seasoning (*I like McCormick*) and/or salt-free multi-spice seasoning

Dried basil

Coconut aminos, liquid aminos, or soy sauce

All-purpose marinade (*I like Over All marinade from RUE Kitchen, but you use what you like*)

Sliced green onions

INSTRUCTIONS

WIPE the mushrooms clean with a damp cloth. If the mushrooms are connected, separate them, and cut any large mushrooms in half. Place them in a large bowl.

PEEL and pit the mango. Slice the flesh into ½-inch-thick strips that are 2 to 3 inches long. Add them to the bowl with the mushrooms.

SPRINKLE the seasoning(s) and basil on top and drizzle in some coconut aminos. Add some marinade and gently toss everything together, making sure that the mushrooms and mango are thoroughly coated in the spices and marinade. Set aside at room temperature for about 1 hour.

HEAT a cast-iron grill pan over medium heat until hot. Use tongs or a slotted spoon to transfer the mushrooms and mango to the grill pan. Cook until browned on both sides, using tongs to flip them over, 3 to 4 minutes per side.

STIR in some of the green onions. Taste and adjust the seasoning. Transfer to a serving platter or plates and top with the remaining green onions. Serve!

Tabism: *Today, wear something fun, and don't apologize for it!*

soups & salads

THERE ARE SO MANY DIFFERENT REASONS I LOVE SOUP. But the number one reason—and I think many share my opinion—is that soup puts me in the cozy mood of the cooler fall and winter seasons. I like to call soups and stews "cuddle food," because I can have a bowl of broccoli cheddar soup or vegan chili while curled up under a blanket on the couch watching my favorite movie. It feels like I'm getting a hug in a bowl. And when it comes to soup's favorite partner—which is salad, of course—I'm a salad girl, through and through. Raw salads are a great way to get lots of nutrients in your body. When you cook any food, the heat kills at least some of the nutrients and vitamins that are naturally in it. But when you eat raw, you ingest all that, and get all the benefits of it.

So any time I can choose a salad, I do. And I hope that any time you can choose a salad, you will. Pair it with a soup for a full meal, or when the rest of the meal is cooked food, add a salad on the side, or replace one meal every day with a fresh salad. Top it with your favorite things, and honey, you cannot go wrong. When you eat plant-based for even just one meal a day, you're doing something great for your body, and you're doing something great for the environment. And listen, it'll feel good going in *and* coming out, if you know what I mean!

Broccoli Cheddar Soup

Before I was vegan, I used to love the broccoli cheddar soup at Panera Bread so much that I knew I needed to figure out how to replicate it at home. And I did. And it was amazing. And then I became vegan and I adapted it to my new lifestyle.

So thank you, Panera, for creating this signature soup that I fell in love with. Then I made my own, and I love it even more!

INGREDIENTS

Fresh or frozen broccoli florets

Shredded or thinly sliced carrots

Vegetable broth

Chopped white onion

Vegan butter

Garlic powder or minced garlic

Smoked paprika

Sea salt

Vegan cheddar cheese shreds (*I like Daiya for this dish*)

Unsweetened plain cashew milk yogurt

FOR SERVING

Vegan croutons (*I like Kelly's Gourmet Cheezy Garlic Croutons*) (optional)

Chopped fresh cilantro or parsley (optional)

INSTRUCTIONS

PUT the broccoli in your food processor and process it until it's very well chopped but there are still a few bigger pieces for texture. Transfer it to a Dutch oven or soup pot.

ADD your carrots and a little broth to the pot and set it over medium-high heat.

ADD your chopped onion and some butter (to add flavor and a smooth texture) and enough broth that the liquid comes up to the level of the vegetables but doesn't cover them. Save a little broth for the end, in case your soup is too thick.

ADD as much garlic powder as you want, a couple pinches of smoked paprika, and a pinch of salt. Go ahead and stir it all together while bringing it to a gentle boil.

REDUCE the heat and boil gently for about 10 minutes, until the vegetables become nice and tender. Can y'all smell that? Oh yes, God have mercy!

ADD the cheddar. Use a lot here, honey. Go on ahead and add the whole bag if your spirit tells you to. Add the yogurt, plus a little more paprika and garlic powder if you want to, because that's your business.

STIR until the cheddar has melted and the yogurt is well blended. If the soup is too thick, add a little of that broth you held back.

REDUCE the heat to medium and simmer for 5 to 7 minutes to let all those flavors dance together. Season to taste.

LADLE it into a bowl, top with some croutons and cilantro or parsley, if you want to, and enjoy!

Tabism: *Hug someone today, starting with yourself! I love you!*

Vegan Chili

Raw pecans

Apple cider vinegar

Garlic powder

Chopped red bell pepper

Chopped green bell pepper

Chopped purple (red) onion

A few drops of liquid smoke

Chili powder

Grapeseed oil

Salt-free seasoning spice, such as red bean and rice seasoning

Raw agave syrup

Canned black beans with the liquid from the can

Canned kidney beans with the liquid from the can

Canned vegetarian baked beans with the liquid from the can

Canned diced tomatoes with their juice

Frozen or fresh corn kernels

Vegetable broth

Brown sugar

Barbecue sauce

Sea salt

Ground black pepper

FOR SERVING

Vegan cheddar cheese shreds

Snipped fresh chives

When I was a young girl, the ladies at the church sold big bowls of chili after Sunday services. It was so very good, and I think that's when I fell in love with chili. When I was a little older and I stopped eating red meat and pork, I still enjoyed a good chili bean soup. But it wasn't until I was grown and living on my own that I discovered good chili made with ground turkey or chicken. And then when I went vegan, I knew I still needed good chili, not only because I like it so much but also because my best friend, Nic—he's like a brother to me—makes the *best* chili. It's almost like a competition between us to see who's making the best chili. He inspires me to keep experimenting and making mine better. I like to say chili is action-packed, because it explodes with flavor in your mouth. The good thing for sure about chili is that you definitely don't need meat to get all that flavor. Just give this one a try and you'll see what I mean.

INSTRUCTIONS

PUT the pecans in a pot and add water to cover along with some apple cider vinegar and garlic powder. Bring to a boil over medium heat, then boil for 12 minutes, until the pecans turn a little lighter in color and soften a little.

DRAIN the pecans and transfer them to a food processor. Add the bell peppers and onion, a few drops of liquid smoke, and a little chili powder. Blend it up. Now you have your base. Doesn't that smell good?

HEAT some oil in a large skillet over medium heat. Add the pecan mixture and sprinkle in a little chili powder, garlic powder, and seasoning spice. Drizzle in a little agave. Sauté for 5 to 7 minutes, stirring every now and then.

MEANWHILE, pour the beans and all the liquid from the cans into a Dutch oven or soup pot set over low heat. Add the tomatoes and all their juice, too. Add the corn.

TRANSFER that pecan "meat" to the pot and pour in just a little broth; you don't need a whole lot of broth, just a little. Stir it all up, turn the heat under the pot up to medium, and bring to a simmer. If you don't see any bubbles at all after a few minutes, turn the heat up a little more.

ADD a couple of sprinkles of brown sugar and a little barbecue sauce. Add your salt and black pepper and stir it all up gently. Give it a taste, and if you want to, sprinkle in a little bit more chili powder.

SIMMER for 20 to 30 minutes, so that everyone can marry each other in the pot. If it gets too thick while it's simmering, stir in a little more broth. Season to taste.

WHEN you're ready, ladle your chili into a bowl. Top with cheddar cheese and fresh chives or a little more of your seasoning, or add all three if you want to and that's your business. Now you can get on into it!

Tabism: *Today I encourage you to try to make a new friend.*

CLOCKWISE
FROM TOP LEFT:
Tortilla Soup, 143;
Spicy Vegetable
Curry Soup, 142; and
Okra Lentil Stew, 141

Okra Lentil Stew

I love okra, and I love lentils, which are a great source of protein. And you know that I like to play in the kitchen, especially when I have not much left in the pantry or refrigerator and don't feel like going to the grocery store. That's when I pull some things together and create something new. That's how this happened. I had on hand two things that I love: okra and lentils. It turns out they love each other, too, and this stew is amazing!

INGREDIENTS

Dried lentils, rinsed

Uncooked rice

Vegan chicken pieces (*I like Quorn Meatless Pieces*)

Sliced fresh or frozen okra

Shredded or sliced carrots

Chopped red bell pepper

Chopped green bell pepper

Canned diced tomatoes with their juice

Chopped sweet onion

Minced garlic

Garlic powder

Salt-free multi-spice seasoning (*whatever your favorite kind is, just add that*)

Dried sage

Sea salt

Ground black pepper

Vegetable broth

INSTRUCTIONS

PUT the lentils, rice, vegan chicken, okra, carrots, bell peppers, tomatoes, onion, and minced garlic in a slow cooker and season with garlic powder, seasoning spice, some sage, salt, and black pepper.

YOU can add all of what I mentioned or just some of it or whatever you've got in your refrigerator or freezer. There ain't no right or wrong, honey—it's your stew, you do it how you want it.

ADD enough broth to come up just to the level of the vegetables but not cover them. Now stir it all up. If you can't see any liquid, add some more broth or water. You want to see all your veggies, but also some liquid right at the surface. Honey, look at the party happening in your pot. All those colors? That's how you know it's good.

COVER and cook on low for 4 to 5 hours, until the lentils and rice are fully cooked and the flavors are combined. Taste and adjust the seasoning.

LADLE into bowls and serve.

Tabism: *Don't be hard on yourself. Just be creative!*

Spicy Vegetable Curry Soup

INGREDIENTS

Red potatoes

Garlic powder

Grapeseed oil

Chopped white onion

Chopped purple (red) onion

Minced garlic

Shredded carrots

Sliced celery

Chopped red, green, and yellow bell peppers

Sliced mushrooms

Dried basil

Salt-free Caribbean seasoning (*I like my Sunshine All Purpose Seasoning from McCormick*)

Salt-free spicy jalapeño seasoning or other spicy seasoning

Crushed red pepper flakes

Kale, stems and ribs removed, leaves chopped

Vegetable broth

Canned coconut cream

Canned diced tomatoes with their juice

Curry powder

Sea salt

I did not grow up eating curry dishes, but today curry is one of my most favorite spice blends. When I first started cooking live online, some people said, "Tab, you're supposed to cook the curry powder in oil before you add anything to it. You ain't cooking it right!" And I said, "Well, you know what? That's how y'all do it. This is the way Tab gonna do it, and it tastes the way I love it."

I always say, you cook your way, and as long as it don't hurt you or kill you, you're all right. My vegetable curry soup tastes very good the way I make it. It's perfect for cold nights during the fall and winter. But to be honest, I will also eat this in the summertime, because that's my business. (Photo on page 140.)

INSTRUCTIONS

PUT the potatoes in a large pot. Cover with water by about 2 inches and add some garlic powder. Bring to a boil over medium-high heat. Reduce the heat and simmer until the potatoes are cooked and tender when pierced with a knife, 10 to 20 minutes, depending on how big they are. Drain and run some cold water over them to cool slightly. Cut them into large dice and set aside.

MEANWHILE, heat some oil in a Dutch oven or large soup pot. Add the onion, garlic, carrots, celery, bell peppers, and mushrooms. Add a little dried basil, Caribbean seasoning, jalapeño seasoning, and crushed red pepper. Sauté, stirring, until the vegetables begin to soften, 5 to 7 minutes.

STIR in some kale and some more garlic powder and sauté another few minutes, until the vegetables are almost fully cooked.

POUR in enough broth to come up to the level of the vegetables but not cover them. Add the coconut cream, the tomatoes with their juice, and the cooked potatoes. Stir and add some curry powder until the spirit tells you to stop and a few pinches of salt.

GIVE it a taste and add more of any seasoning you think it needs. Is there enough kick for you? If not, add some more spice.

INCREASE the heat and bring the soup to a simmer. When everything is hot all the way through, you're ready to serve!

Tabism: *Don't pay negative energy no mind, because it's certainly not paying you.*

Tortilla Soup

INGREDIENTS

Grapeseed oil

Minced garlic

Sliced oyster mushrooms

Salt-free seasoning spice

Adobo seasoning*

Dried cilantro

Chopped purple (red) onion

Chopped yellow and red bell peppers

Fresh cilantro leaves

Canned diced tomatoes with their juice

Canned black beans with the liquid from the can

Vegan no-chicken broth or vegetable broth

Fresh limes

Fresh or frozen corn kernels (*if you want*)

FOR SERVING

Vegan cheese shreds

Sliced avocado

Tortilla chips

Pico de Gallo (page 60)

Remember—when using any seasoning that contains salt, don't be heavy-handed!

When I first moved to California I worked at Macy's in Century City, and most days I ate lunch at Baja Fresh in the food court. I would get their tortilla soup because I thought it was amazing. I'd never had it before, because I never really ate Mexican food growing up. All we had was Taco Bell, which was where I worked my first job. We didn't have tortilla soup, and if we did, it sure wasn't that!

After trying it for the first time at Baja Fresh, when I would go to authentic Mexican restaurants, I would be so excited to try their versions, with real chicken in those days. And it just became a favorite soup of mine, especially living here in Los Angeles, where we are lucky to have so many places to get delicious tortilla soup. So when I became vegan, I knew I was going to have to figure out how to make it at home, because I still had to have it. And I did, and I do. And honey, it's very, very good. (Photo on page 140.)

INSTRUCTIONS

HEAT some oil in a large sauté pan over medium heat. Add the garlic, mushrooms, seasoning spice, adobo seasoning, and dried cilantro. Sauté, stirring occasionally, until the mushrooms are lightly browned.

STIR in the onion, bell peppers, and some fresh cilantro leaves and sauté, stirring occasionally, until the vegetables are softened.

POUR the diced tomatoes with their juice and the beans with the liquid from the can into a Dutch oven or soup pot. Add enough broth to just cover the tomatoes and beans. Bring to a simmer over medium heat.

SQUEEZE the juice of a lime into the sauté pan, then scrape the vegetables into the pot with the tomato-bean mixture. Add the corn, if you're using it, and some more fresh cilantro leaves. Taste and add some more of whatever seasoning you think it needs.

SIMMER for 10 to 15 minutes so all the flavors come together. Taste and adjust the seasoning.

TO serve, ladle the soup into bowls. Top with cheese shreds, avocado slices, tortilla chips, and pico de gallo. Get *into* that soup!

Tabism: *Drink a hot herbal tea today. Sip slow and allow yourself to feel the warmth take over your body.*

Okra, Bell Pepper, and Cucumber Salad

Some people don't like okra because of its sliminess, but when okra is raw, it isn't really slimy at all. It's crunchy and delicious. I love raw okra so much that I was inspired to create this salad around it. Eating raw vegetables is so healthy because when you don't cook them, they retain all their nutrients and enzymes. Several times a year, I do a week or more of eating only raw food, and I always feel amazing. Maybe you can join me during a raw-diet week sometime? And bring this salad with you, please!

INGREDIENTS

Sliced fresh okra

Chopped red bell pepper

Chopped mini cucumber

Chopped purple (red) onion

Apple cider vinegar

Extra-virgin olive oil

Low-salt or salt-free garlic and herb seasoning blend (*I like Cooking with Greens Pink Himalayan Go To Blend for this salad, but you use what you like*)

INSTRUCTIONS

PLACE the okra, bell peppers, cucumbers, and onions in a large bowl. Pour in a little vinegar and drizzle in a little oil. Add a few shakes of seasoning blend and stir it all up. You're ready to eat!

IF you have any leftovers the next day, you can stuff those in an avocado half. You're going to look like you're fancy *and* eat real good!

Tabism: *Drink or eat something raw, pure, and green today, and be excited about what it's going to do for your body!*

Vegan Cobb Salad

Before my husband became vegan, he absolutely loved a true Cobb salad, which includes things like chicken, bacon, and eggs. Of course, those things are not on the menu in the Brown family kitchen anymore, but this vegan Cobb salad definitely is! (Photo on page 153.)

INGREDIENTS

Mixed greens, including baby kale

Chopped mushrooms (*you can use pickled mushrooms if your spirit tells you that's the right thing to do*)

Chopped fresh tomato

Chopped cucumber

Diced avocado

Vegan cheddar cheese shreds

Vegan bacon bits

Vegan crouton crumbs (*I like Kelly's Just Crumbs*) or whole vegan croutons, if that's what you have

Vegan deli slices (*use whichever version you like*), chopped

Your favorite vegan vinaigrette, or oil and vinegar

INSTRUCTIONS

SPREAD the greens in a large shallow bowl or on a platter. Arrange each ingredient on top of the greens, either in piles or in rows: mushrooms, tomato, cucumber, avocado, cheese, bacon bits, crouton crumbs, and chopped deli slices.

WHEN you're ready to serve the salad, drizzle the vinaigrette over the whole thing, or let people dress their own after they've served themselves (do it this way if you think you're going to have leftovers; they'll keep better if they're not dressed).

Tabism: *It's okay to take a break.*

Tab's Favorite Salad

There are so many colors and textures in this salad, and with the beans for extra protein it's definitely a full meal. And you know that this has dill pickles in it, one of my favorite things of all. What's that, you're asking? Why are there pickles in the salad? Well, honey, because this is my favorite salad, and that's my business. You can leave them out if you don't like them, and that's your business.

INGREDIENTS

Mixed greens

Chopped red bell pepper

Chopped white mushrooms

Chopped cucumber

Chopped drained dill pickles

Cooked or canned red kidney beans, drained and rinsed

Roughly chopped fresh cilantro leaves

Dried cranberries

Chopped pecans

FOR SERVING

Vegan croutons (*I like Kelly's Gourmet Cheezy Garlic Croutons*)

Kelly's Lemon Pepper Parm or other seasoning

Sea salt

Ground black pepper

Your favorite vegan vinaigrette

INSTRUCTIONS

PUT your mixed greens in a large bowl. Add your bell pepper, mushrooms, cucumber, pickles, beans, cilantro, cranberries, and pecans. Use tongs to gently toss all the ingredients together.

ADD the croutons and lemon pepper parm and a pinch each of salt and pepper. Drizzle your vinaigrette on top and toss to coat all the ingredients. Season with more salt, pepper, or lemon pepper parm to your taste.

NOW *that's* a salad!

Tabism: *Taste the rainbow and know that you are more precious than a pot of gold!*

SOUPS & SALADS   147

Chopped Salad

Chopped salad shows how we can change everything just by approaching our ingredients a little differently. All the components in this salad could be prepared more or less like every other salad in this chapter. Everything could just be thinly sliced or chopped, and you'd have a very pretty, delicious salad. But when we put those same ingredients in a food processor or blender and chop them fine, we get a little bit of everything in every single bite, and it just tastes better. It's a completely different experience than when only two or three different elements can fit on your fork at one time.

Isn't that like life? Sometimes things are great as they are, but sometimes, when you mix everything up together, it's even more fun, and we get a lot more joy out of it.

INGREDIENTS

Kale, stems and ribs removed

Mixed greens

Brussels sprouts, cut in half

Red bell pepper, cut into quarters

Sweet onion, cut into thin wedges

Apple, cut into quarters and cored

Jarred artichoke hearts, including some of their liquid

Walnuts or pecans

Golden raisins

Apple cider vinegar

Fresh lime juice

Extra-virgin olive oil

Garlic powder and any other seasonings you like

Sliced avocado

Sea salt

Ground black pepper

INSTRUCTIONS

YOU'RE going to let your food processor or blender do all the hard work here. Just make sure not to overfill it; you can do just one or two ingredients at a time if you'd like, and combine them all in a large bowl as you go.

IN your food processor or blender, combine the kale, mixed greens, Brussels sprouts, bell pepper, onion, apple, artichoke hearts (plus a little of the liquid from their jar), nuts, and raisins.

POUR in a little vinegar. Squeeze in the juice of a lime. Drizzle some oil on top, and sprinkle in some garlic powder and any other seasonings you want.

PROCESS or blend until the ingredients are finely chopped but not mushy, stopping the machine and using a spatula to stir a few times. It's fine if there are some bigger bits, honey.

TRANSFER the salad to a big bowl. Taste and adjust the seasoning.

PUT the sliced avocado on top. Season with a pinch each of salt and black pepper and serve!

Tabism: *Today, eat a few raisins. They are small but mighty and full of fiber!!*

Kale and Raspberry Salad

When I was growing up, nobody ate kale raw. And when we said we were eating salad, honey, we were talking about cooked greens. That was a whole different type of salad, right? I mean, we *had* raw salads, but we called it something different—we called it "toss salad." So I never ate raw kale until I moved to Los Angeles. I was like, "You mean these cooked greens I've been eating all this time (and calling a salad) I can eat *raw* (and call it a salad)?"

I knew nothing about "massaging" kale until I became vegan. The first time I heard someone say something about it, I was like, "What do you mean you 'massage the kale'? Like, you *massage* it, massage it?"

That feels like a long time ago. Now I can tell you that massaging raw kale just means you rub it between your fingers and hands with some oil and seasonings. This softens the leaves and makes them tasty and easier to chew and digest. Massaged kale is a great base for a salad, and it is especially good mixed with fresh fruit like the raspberries here; the sweetness and juice they add is a really nice contrast to the hearty kale.

INGREDIENTS

Kale, stems and ribs removed

Extra-virgin olive oil

Fresh lemon juice

Sea salt

Ground black pepper

Fresh raspberries

Sliced sweet onion

Sliced red bell pepper

Diced avocado

INSTRUCTIONS

WASH the kale and dry it well. Chop or tear the leaves into small pieces and put them in a large bowl.

DRIZZLE on some oil and lemon juice; not too much, just enough to moisten the leaves. Remember, you can always add more, but you can't take it back out.

ADD a pinch each of salt and black pepper.

NOW use your hands to give that kale a massage, rubbing the oil and lemon juice into the leaves. Kale is tough, so you can really get on into it, honey. Keep massaging the kale for about 5 minutes, until it all looks shiny and the color is a little darker than it was.

ADD the raspberries, onion, bell pepper, and avocado. Toss gently to combine. Season to taste, then serve!

Tabism: *Smile—you have chosen to try something new today!*

Beet Salad

I absolutely love beets. I know that not everyone feels the same way, but I wish everyone did. Beets are so very good for all of us, and in people with high blood pressure, they can actually reduce blood pressure! They're an amazing food, and they deserve to be the star of this beautiful salad.

INGREDIENTS

Mixed greens

Sliced white onion

Shredded carrots

Sliced red bell pepper

Sliced cucumber

Pickled beets, drained and sliced

Pepitas (pumpkin seeds)

Vegan parmesan cheese shreds

Everything bagel seasoning* (*I like McCormick*)

Your favorite vegan salad dressing (*I like Newman's Own White Balsamic Vinaigrette*)

Remember—when using any seasoning that contains salt, don't be heavy-handed!

INSTRUCTIONS

PUT the mixed greens in a large bowl or on a platter.

ARRANGE the onion, carrots, bell pepper, cucumber, and beets on top and sprinkle on the pepitas and parmesan.

ADD some everything bagel seasoning and drizzle with salad dressing. Toss and season to taste.

BABY, we done. OOHHH, GOD, WE THANK YOU. Let's eat!

Tabism: *Are you hurt, or injured? Know the difference.*

Vegan Cobb
Salad, 146

Beet Salad,
152

Rainbow Salad

I remember when "rainbow salads" became a thing a few years ago. I loved beautiful, colorful salads even before they got their own marketing campaign, so I was already there!

INGREDIENTS

Mixed greens

Kale, stems and ribs removed, leaves chopped

Sliced or chopped yellow and orange bell peppers

Sliced or chopped purple (red) onion

Chopped tomato

Sliced or chopped cucumber

Sliced black olives

Sliced or cubed avocado

Dried cranberries

Sunflower seeds

Sea salt

Ground black pepper

Your favorite vegan zesty Italian or balsamic salad dressing, for serving

INSTRUCTIONS

IN a large bowl, combine the mixed greens, kale, bell peppers, onion, tomato, cucumber, and black olives. Gently toss the ingredients together.

SPRINKLE on the avocado, dried cranberries, and sunflower seeds. Season with a pinch of salt and some black pepper.

DRIZZLE on your favorite dressing and taste for seasoning. Serve up your rainbow in a bowl!

Tabism: *Stop apologizing for winning!*

Warm Lobster Mushroom Salad

It's no secret that I love mushrooms, and one of the ways I love to use them is on top of my salad, especially ones with dark leafy greens like spinach and kale. These darker greens are hearty and can hold their own with something as flavorful as warm mushrooms. And when you top those greens with some warm *lobster mushrooms*? Honey, you feel like you're having a whole lobster salad! That's because their red color looks like a cooked lobster shell, and their flavor and firm texture are even a little like that of real seafood.

INGREDIENTS

Fresh lobster mushrooms or other meaty mushrooms

Vegan butter

Nori komi furikake seasoning

Garlic powder

Coconut aminos, liquid aminos, or soy sauce

Chili-garlic sauce (*I like Huy Fong*)

Mixed greens, including some dark leafy greens like spinach and baby kale, collards, or mustard greens

Your favorite vegan salad dressing (*I like Newman's Own White Balsamic Vinaigrette*)

INSTRUCTIONS

WIPE the mushrooms clean with a damp cloth. Trim and slice them, then set aside.

COMBINE the butter, nori komi furikake, garlic powder, coconut aminos, and chili-garlic sauce in a glass measuring cup. Microwave until the butter is melted.

MEANWHILE, put the mushrooms in a nonstick skillet with a tight-fitting lid. Place the pan over medium heat. Stir the melted butter sauce to blend it, then pour it over the mushrooms, making sure they're evenly coated. Oohhh, do you smell that? Oh my God!

WHEN the sauce starts to bubble, cover the pan and cook for 10 minutes to soften and cook the mushrooms down a bit.

PUT your greens in a serving bowl. Arrange the mushrooms on top of the greens. Drizzle some salad dressing on top. Taste, adjust the seasoning, and serve!

Tabism: *Today, eat something red, and enjoy every bite!*

sweet treats & fresh juices

I'm not a big dessert person. I'm not one of those people who wakes up in the morning and thinks, *Oohhh, I want to bake a cake today.* That ain't my thing. Plus, baking requires measurements, and I like cooking from the spirit. However, when I have a sugar craving, I have a few recipes that do the trick! So here's my collection of treats, including juices, which can really hit the spot when you want something sweet and are eating extra healthy. I'm putting these at the end of my cookbook because desserts typically come last, even though I think you can eat or drink these pretty much any time of day. But if you want to make them for dessert, honey, you do that, because it's your business, and nobody can tell you otherwise.

Lazy Peach Cobbler

My girlfriend Catarah Coleman is like a sister to me. She's also an amazing baker and the co-owner of Southern Girl Desserts, the renowned Los Angeles bakery. A few years ago, she brought a peach cobbler to Thanksgiving dinner. Honey, that cobbler looked and smelled so good. I was still new to being vegan, and I asked about it. She was like, "Oh my God, sis. I'm so sorry, honey. You can't eat that." She is a traditional baker, and that means butter and eggs, but right away she said she would figure out a way to make it vegan for me.

And she did. Not only that, she volunteered to come over to my house to show me how to make it myself. Of course we did a video together, and it was so much fun, and the cobbler is so delicious. But the truly great thing about a *lazy* peach cobbler is that it doesn't require a whole lot of work. And that's right up Tab's alley, because I don't have that kind of time!

So this one is for all the folks out there like me who ain't got baking in their ministry and who ain't got time to be doing a whole lot of baking but still want to be able to serve their family and friends something that's tasty and sweet—and that *looks* like it took a lot of work. (We'll all just keep that part a secret, right?)

INGREDIENTS

Coconut or avocado oil spray, for the pan

1 cup self-rising flour

½ cup sugar

Pinch of ground cinnamon (*add a little more if you want more, honey*)

One 7.4-ounce can condensed coconut milk

1 stick (8 tablespoons) vegan butter, melted

One 29-ounce can sliced peaches in heavy syrup

1 teaspoon pure vanilla extract

INSTRUCTIONS

PREHEAT the oven to 350°F. Spray the bottom and sides of a 9- or 10-inch deep-dish pie plate or square baking pan with oil.

IN a medium bowl, whisk together the flour, sugar, and cinnamon. Add the condensed milk and use a spoon to stir until no more bits of flour are visible and the ingredients come together to form a dough (this is a workout for your arm, honey).

POUR the melted butter into the prepared pie plate. Make sure the butter covers the bottom.

TRANSFER the dough to the pie plate. You can spread it out a little, but don't worry about it if you don't feel like it. The oven is going to do most of the hard work for us.

POUR the peaches with their syrup on top of the dough. Pour the vanilla on top, and add a little more cinnamon there if you want to.

BAKE until the peaches are browned on top and the crust is golden brown, 50 minutes to 1 hour. (Slide a sheet pan onto the rack below the cobbler while it bakes to catch any juices.)

HONEY. Do you see and smell what the good Lord has done here?! Let it cool for a few minutes before scooping out servings so you don't burn your tongue off!

Tabism: *Sometimes you need a day to do absolutely nothing. We all need to recharge sometimes.*

Strawberry (or Blueberry) Cheesecake Cups

So this is how cheesecake conversations happen with my son:

Tab: So, Quest, what is it that we love about strawberry cheesecake?

Quest: Well, first, I like the whipped cream on it, obviously. Second, it is very good. It also . . . I don't even think it has cheese on it.

Tab: Right, we use cashews and make it vegan. Because you don't like cheese, but you like vegan cheese, right? So back in the day when you first really had strawberry cheesecake, where was it?

Quest: At the, er, factory?

Tab: Yep, the Cheesecake Factory. It was a place that our family would go often when you were a baby. And even before you were born, on maybe a Saturday or Sunday or sometimes with family and friends we'd go. And Daddy and I would always get a couple pieces of strawberry cheesecake to go, and we'd eat it when we got home.

Quest: But now you can't because you're vegan.

Tab: That's right. And I'm also allergic to dairy, so now I make the vegan version. But first I had to figure out how to do it. And this was very early on in my vegan journey, back when I would go online to learn what other people were doing. So I explored cashew cheesecake and raw desserts and things like that. And then of course I made it my own and started adding strawberries and blueberries to it and making different versions. And you all love it.

Quest: It's very good.

Tab: Oh, it is very good. So you know, when you're making vegan cheesecakes, the fun part about it is that you can throw in whatever fruit you want. That's the great thing about cooking with only fruits and vegetables. We can just throw them into things and see how it turns out.

Quest: Like cucumbers?

Tab: Ha ha, I don't know about that! But you know you just blend everything together here, and once you freeze it, you get everything in one delicious bite. I really do enjoy this recipe, because it's so quick, and you ain't ever got to turn on nobody's stove.

Quest: It's just natural. It just taste good to your tongue and is like *chef's kiss*.

Tab: Another kid-approved dish! Okay! Very good.

INGREDIENTS

For about 2 servings

1 or 2 vegan graham crackers or Oreo cookies (filling scraped out) for each glass

Raw agave syrup

1 or 2 handfuls of raw cashews

One 5- or 6-ounce container vanilla cashew milk yogurt or other plant-based yogurt

Vanilla cashew milk or other plant-based milk, as needed

3 avocado slices

Sliced strawberries and/ or blueberries (*fresh or frozen, it's up to you, but even when I use frozen in the blended part, I like fresh on top*)

Vegan whipped cream or dessert topping

INSTRUCTIONS

PULL out however many glasses you want to use. What size glass, you ask? Well, honey, how big do you want each serving to be? I use pretty, clear plastic cups that are around 8 to 10 ounces. You use whatever you have.

USE your hands or a spoon (or both) to crush one or two graham crackers or Oreos into the bottom of each glass. Squeeze a little agave on top and set the glasses aside.

PUT the cashews in a Ninja or blender. Add the yogurt, a splash of milk, avocado, and a few slices of strawberry or a few blueberries or both, honey. Blend until smooth, adding another splash or two of milk, if necessary, to keep it moving in the machine. You want it to be thick, though, so don't overdo it.

SPOON the custard into the glasses. Or pipe it into the glasses using a pastry bag fitted with a wide tip, if you have that sort of thing in your kitchen. I do not, so I use a spoon or a spatula or both.

COVER the glasses with aluminum foil or plastic wrap and freeze for at least 45 minutes so they get nice and cold. You can leave them in the freezer as long as you want, honey, up to a few days, but 45 minutes is the least amount of time I freeze them. (If they're frozen solid, let them sit at room temperature for an hour or two so they can soften up.)

JUST before serving, spoon on some whipped cream and top with sliced strawberries or whole blueberries or both.

Tabism: *Have a slice of (vegan) cake and celebrate yourself!*

Chocolate Banana Toast

Listen, honey, Chance has a sweet tooth. One night he was craving something sweet, and we had nothing in the house. So I just got creative with a few things I knew he loves, and I made him some toast and topped it with chocolate hummus and bananas. It was just to curb his appetite, you know, to get that sweet tooth satisfied, but he loved it. And then Quest tried it, and he loved it, too, so it became an occasional family dessert, and sometimes I top it with strawberries for some extra color. And now when my friends come over and we're playing cards in the middle of the night or something, and they want something sweet, I go in there and I hook everybody up with this and everybody loves it.

Oh, and if it looks like a breakfast to you, go on and serve it in the morning instead of for dessert. (Photo on page 168.)

INGREDIENTS

Vegan cinnamon raisin bread, such as Dave's Killer Bread Raisin' the Roof! (*it's not labeled vegan, but it is*)

Vegan chocolate hummus spread

Banana

Ground cinnamon

Sliced strawberries (*if you want them*)

Pure maple syrup

Powdered sugar

INSTRUCTIONS

TOAST two slices of bread.

SPREAD some chocolate hummus on one side of each piece of toast.

SLICE the banana. Arrange a layer of banana on top of the chocolate hummus on one of the pieces of toast.

SPRINKLE a little cinnamon on top. Put the other piece of toast on top, chocolate-side down. Cut the sandwich in half diagonally.

PUT the two halves on a plate. Top with sliced strawberries, if you'd like. Drizzle the whole thing with a little maple syrup and sprinkle with some powdered sugar. Eat with a fork and knife or out of your hand if you don't mind getting a little sticky. Either way you choose is your business.

Tabism: *Today, treat yourself to something sweet, because it's your business, honey.*

Smoothie Bowl

So this is a delicious, healthy dessert, or snack, or dinner, if that's your business. It's just a great way to get a lot of nourishing fruit and fiber (and even protein, if you top it with hemp granola) into your body without overthinking it. You just feel like you're eating something that tastes good. Even the kids love them. Choyce has loved smoothie bowls since she was little, and Quest loves them so much, he tries to get me to make them two or three times a week! So make yourself and your family a good old smoothie bowl, honey, and then sit down with them for a pair of seconds and enjoy that precious time together. (Photo on page 169.)

INGREDIENTS

Frozen bananas

Frozen blueberries

Peanut butter

Spinach

Vanilla almond milk or other plant-based milk

Raw agave syrup

Ground cinnamon

FOR THE TOPPING

Shaved coconut

Granola

Sliced strawberries

Raw agave syrup

INSTRUCTIONS

PUT your frozen fruit, peanut butter, and spinach in a blender. Add a splash or two of milk, a drizzle of agave, and a dash of cinnamon—or two or three dashes, if you'd like.

BLEND everything together until smooth; if it's not blending easily, add a little more milk to loosen it up a bit (but don't add too much milk, because then you're making a smoothie and not a smoothie *bowl*). Transfer to a bowl.

TOP with shaved coconut, granola, and sliced strawberries. Drizzle some agave over it all.

AND now do you see what you've made? You've made yourself a whole bowl of sunshine. Go on now and get into it!

Tabism: *It's hard to cross back over a burned bridge.*

Fresh Juices

There are so many fresh juice combinations that I love, that I could probably do a whole book full of just juices.

Honey. That's a good idea! But in the meantime, here are a few juices that I'm enjoying most right now. Just remember to choose what fruits and veggies you juice based on what *you* enjoy. For instance, in the Refresh, if you really love watermelon, use much more of that and just a few strawberries. Or if you love lime, go ahead and add more of it. There are no rules, but I know for sure that the combinations here are delicious.

Carrot-Apple-Ginger

I always juice the carrots first before I juice the apple and ginger and then set the carrot pulp aside to use in the filling for my very delicious Spicy Tuna Roll (page 79).

Several carrots
1 red or green apple
Thumb-size piece of fresh ginger
Pinch of ground cinnamon (optional)

Pineapple-Cucumber

A tropical paradise, all in the push of the blender button.

½ of a large pineapple
1 large cucumber
Fresh mint to taste

Pear Pie Delight

This is one of my favorite juice recipes, especially for those with a sweet tooth!

1 sweet potato or yam
1 red or green apple
1 yellow or Asian pear
Handful of blueberries
Pinch of ground cinnamon

Pain Blaster

Pain is temporary. I believe we have the power to live pain-free, and sometimes the right juice combo can jump-start the journey.

1 large orange
Thumb-size piece of fresh turmeric
Pinch of ground black pepper

LEFT TO RIGHT:
Pain Blaster, 171;
Carrot Apple-Ginger,
171; Refresh, 173; Pear
Pie Delight, 171; and
Pineapple-Cucumber, 171

Refresh

We can all use a refresher moment, and right now, it's your time.

¼ to ½ of a small watermelon
Fresh mint to taste
Handful of strawberries
1 lime

Cherry-Apple

Did someone say candy apple in juice form? Well, this gives you all the vibes, with a sour twist.

1 red or green apple
Handful of pitted sweet cherries
1 lime

Tabism: *Fruit is God's candy.*

Holy Green Juice

In church when you take Communion you use grape juice. And when we add a little kale and lime to the grape, we get holy green juice—Amen!

Handful of kale
Handful of green grapes
1 lime

Grapefruit-Pineapple

You know how grapefruit can be bitter and pineapple can be very sweet? Well, even though sometimes life can be bittersweet, it can still be delicious.

1 grapefruit
Handful of chopped pineapple
Fresh mint to taste

Menus for Gathering

I like to let my spirit guide me when I'm thinking about what to serve my family and friends. Whether it's a special occasion or a regular weeknight, I always think of who I'm preparing food for. I get super excited to surprise them with things that I know they will love. I let them and my spirit inspire me. But I know that sometimes we can all use a little help with inspiration, so here are a few ideas based on the recipes in this book!

Game Day

Valentine's Day

Mother's Day Brunch

Memorial Day/Juneteenth/ Fourth of July/Labor Day BBQ

Holiday

Weeknight Dinners

Universal Conversion Chart

OVEN TEMPERATURE EQUIVALENTS

250°F = 120°C

275°F = 135°C

300°F = 150°C

325°F = 160°C

350°F = 180°C

375°F = 190°C

400°F = 200°C

425°F = 220°C

450°F = 230°C

475°F = 240°C

500°F = 260°C

MEASUREMENT EQUIVALENTS

Measurements should always be level unless directed otherwise.

⅛ teaspoon = 0.5 mL

¼ teaspoon = 1 mL

½ teaspoon = 2 mL

1 teaspoon = 5 mL

1 tablespoon = 3 teaspoons = ½ fluid ounce = 15 mL

2 tablespoons = ⅛ cup = 1 fluid ounce = 30 mL

4 tablespoons = ¼ cup = 2 fluid ounces = 60 mL

5⅓ tablespoons = ⅓ cup = 3 fluid ounces = 80 mL

8 tablespoons = ½ cup = 4 fluid ounces = 120 mL

10⅔ tablespoons = ⅔ cup = 5 fluid ounces = 160 mL

12 tablespoons = ¾ cup = 6 fluid ounces = 180 mL

16 tablespoons = 1 cup = 8 fluid ounces = 240 mL

Acknowledgments

DEAR GOD, THANK YOU FOR TRUSTING ME WITH THIS JOURNEY! Thank you for whispering in my ear and telling me to share what I'm eating with the world! Thank you, Chance, for being a Southern man who is always hungry—because of you, I learned my way around the kitchen! Thank you for eating the terrible meals in 1998 and 1999; I hope I've made up for those days now. Thank you, Moma, Granny, and Aunt Diane, aka "Sista," who taught me how to cook over the phone—we've come a long way, honey! Thank you to my children, who keep their opinions honest and are never shy about their requests for their favorite meals! I love y'all so much!

To my fans, especially those of you from Facebook who started with me in the room, I can't ever thank you enough for sticking by my side all these years. Your support is everything to me—thank you so very much!

To my Scale Management team, thank you for keeping my life and schedule together so I could finish this project. To my agents at CAA, Cindy Uh and Carlos Segarra, I honestly can't imagine ever writing a book without you both. You are seriously my secret weapon, and I appreciate you both so very much!

To Cassie Jones, my editor, and the whole William Morrow/HarperCollins team, thank you for letting me be me and literally make a cookbook without traditional measurements. It means so much to me that you all see me and believe in me! I love you all!

Matt Armendariz, the way you and your team bring life to my food through pictures is mind-blowing, and I am so thankful we did this together! Thank you!!

Marah Stets, there really aren't words to describe how grateful I am that you said yes to helping me on this journey! I could not have done it without you! I'm so sorry for all my late-night voice notes and messages. I'm wishing you tons of uninterrupted sleep for the next year. Seriously, thank you so much for embracing my nontraditional ways and taking this journey with me—I love you, honey!

May we all spend fun times cooking from the spirit!

Index

NOTE: Page numbers in *italics* indicate photos or photo captions.

HarperCollins books may be purchased for educational, business, or sales promotional use. For information, please email the Special Markets Department at SPsales@harpercollins.com.

FIRST EDITION

DESIGNED BY RENATA DE OLIVEIRA
ALL PHOTOGRAPHS BY MATT ARMENDARIZ

Lace pattern by gudimm/Shutterstock

Library of Congress Cataloging-in-Publication Data has been applied for.

ISBN 978-0-06-308032-4

22 23 24 25 26 LSC 10 9 8 7 6 5 4 3 2 1